EARLY PEOPLES

ANCIENT ROMANS

WORLD
BOOK

World Book
a Scott Fetzer company
Chicago
www.worldbookonline.com

World Book, Inc.
233 N. Michigan Avenue
Chicago, IL 60601
U.S.A.

For information about other World Book publications, visit our Web site at
http://www.worldbookonline.com or call 1-800-WORLDBK (967-5325).
For information about sales to schools and libraries, call 1-800-975-3250
(United States), or 1-800-837-5365 (Canada).

Library of Congress Cataloging-in-Publication Data

Ancient Romans.
    p. cm. -- (Early peoples)
    Includes index.
    Summary: "A discussion of the early Romans, including who
  the people were, where they lived, the rise of civilization, social
  structure, religion, art and architecture, science and technology,
  daily life, entertainment and sports. Features include timelines,
  fact boxes, glossary, list of recommended reading and Web sites,
  and index"--Provided by publisher.
    ISBN 978-0-7166-2131-7
    1. Rome--Civilization--Juvenile literature. I. World Book, Inc.
  DG77.A58 2009
  937--dc22
                                            2008039352

Printed in China
1 2 3 4 5 13 12 11 10 09

STAFF

TABLE OF CONTENTS

WHO WERE THE ANCIENT ROMANS?   4-5

ORIGINS   6-7

FROM REPUBLIC TO EMPIRE   8-9

CONSULS AND EMPERORS   10-11

PATRICIANS AND PLEBEIANS   12-13

THE ARMY   14-15

WOMEN   16-17

FARMERS   18-19

SLAVES AND FREED SLAVES   20-21

LAW, CRIME, AND PUNISHMENT   22-23

BELIEFS AND GODS   24-25

PRIESTS AND CEREMONIES   26-27

THE ROMAN CALENDAR   28-29

ROMAN ARCHITECTURE   30-31

ENGINEERING AND SCIENCE   32-33

THE BUILDINGS OF
    ANCIENT ROME   34-35

PAINTINGS, MOSAICS, AND
    SCULPTURES   36-37

METAL, GLASS, AND POTTERY   38-39

LITERATURE AND LIBRARIES   40-41

POMPEII   42-43

FAMILY LIFE AND CHILDREN   44-45

CLOTHING   46-47

ROADS AND TRANSPORTATION   48-49

FOOD   50-51

SPORT AND SPECTACLE   52-53

THEATER, MUSIC, AND DANCE   54-55

DECLINE AND FALL   56-57

THE ROMAN LEGACY   58-59

GLOSSARY   60-61

ADDITIONAL RESOURCES   62

INDEX   63-64

Glossary There is a glossary on pages 60-61. Terms defined in the glossary are in type **that looks like this** on their first appearance on any spread (two facing pages).

Additional Resources Books for further reading and recommended Web sites are listed on page 62. Because of the nature of the Internet, some Web site addresses may have changed since publication. The publisher has no responsibility for any such changes or for the content of cited sources.

WHO WERE THE ANCIENT ROMANS?

Around 3,000 years ago, a small community of **Latin** farmers lived along the banks of the Tiber *(TY buhr)* River in present-day central Italy, in a region called Latium *(LAT ee um)*. Over the following centuries, the descendants of this small community went on to create one of the greatest **empires** in history—the Roman Empire. The Romans took their name from the city of Rome, which, according to their **legends**, was founded in 753 B.C., though evidence uncovered by **archaeologists** suggests that the city emerged around 600 B.C. The Romans gained control over more and more of the territory that made up the Italian peninsula until, by 272 B.C., most of this region was under the control of the Roman **Republic**. By the A.D. 100's, the Romans had conquered a vast empire that extended into three continents— Europe, Asia, and Africa.

The Romans created their empire by conquering territories with their well-disciplined and fearsome army. Once a territory was under their control, however, the Romans built roads and towns, and they spread the Roman way of life. At the height of the empire, people from Britain in the north to Egypt in the south dressed like Romans, lived in Roman-style houses, and worshiped Roman gods. Roman government, conquest, and culture had a profound

▲ The Colosseum *(KOL uh SEE uhm)*, a giant **amphitheate**r *(AM fuh thee uh tuhr)*, in Rome, was completed in A.D. 80 to stage huge and expensive public spectacles. The ruins of the Colosseum are visited by thousands of tourists every year.

influence on the Western world. This influence survives today in the languages spoken in many countries, in architecture and engineering, and in Western legal and political systems.

The Roman World

The Italian peninsula juts out into the Mediterranean (*MEHD uh tuh RAY nee uhn*) Sea. To the north lie the Alps, a rugged mountain range that provided a natural defense against invaders from central Europe. However, the Romans gradually extended their control far beyond the Italian peninsula to all the lands that bordered the Mediterranean.

The Founding of Rome

According to Roman legend, the city of Rome was founded by twin brothers named Romulus and Remus (*ROM yuh luhs* and *REE muhs*). The twins had been abandoned as babies. A she-wolf cared for the infants until they were rescued by a shepherd, who brought them up as his own children. When Romulus and Remus set out to found the city, they argued about where it should be built. The dispute ended with the death of Remus, and so Romulus named the city *Rome*, for himself.

▼ A **bronze** sculpture of a she-wolf nursing the twins Romulus and Remus, the legendary founders of Rome. The she-wolf in this sculpture has recently been dated to the A.D. 1200's. The figures of the twins were added in the 1500's. Until recently, the sculpture was believed to be much older.

TIMELINE OF ANCIENT ROME

753 B.C.	Legendary founding of Rome by Romulus and Remus
509 B.C.	Romans establish the Roman Republic
272 B.C.	Rome extends its rule to virtually the entire Italian peninsula
264–146 B.C.	Rome begins overseas expansion by defeating Carthage (*KAHR thihj*) in the three Punic (*PYOO nihk*) Wars
44 B.C.	**Dictator** Julius Caesar (*SEE zuhr*) is assassinated by Roman aristocrats as he enters the **Senate** on March 15 (the Ides of March)
27 B.C.	Octavian (*ok TAY vee uhn*) becomes the first Roman emperor and takes the name Augustus (*aw GUHS thus*); he begins expanding the Empire
27 B.C.– A.D. 180	Pax Romana—period of peace and stability in the Roman Empire
A.D. 98–117	Under the Emperor Trajan (*TRAY juhn*), the Roman Empire reaches its greatest size
A.D. 325	Constantine (*KON stuhn TEEN*) makes Christianity the chief religion of the Roman Empire
A.D. 395	Roman Empire is permanently divided into two parts, the West Roman Empire and the East Roman Empire
A.D. 476	Last emperor of the West Roman Empire is overthrown

ORIGINS

The **Latins** were one of several groups of people living on the Italian
peninsula during the first millennium B.C. (the thousand-year
period that began in 1000 B.C.). In the countryside east of the Tiber
River lived the **Sabines** *(SAY bynz);* and to the south were the **Samnites**
(SAM nytz). The ancient Greeks had founded a number of **colonies** along
the coasts of what is today southern Italy and Sicily, and people from
Carthage in North Africa had settled in what is present-day northwest
Sicily. The north of the Italian peninsula was dominated by the **Etruscans**
(ih TRUHS kuhnz), who established a **civilization** based around powerful
city-states, each one ruled by a king.

Early Rome

Rome was founded on seven hills, and the earliest settlement in Rome was
on the Palatine *(PAL uh tin)* Hill—the centermost of the seven. The
Romans drained and paved the marshy land between the Palatine and
another of Rome's hills, the Capitoline *(KA put uhl in)*, to create a public
area that later became Rome's **Forum**. They also built roads and public
buildings. Both the Etruscans and the Romans traded extensively with the
Greeks to the south. Rome prospered and grew under the rule of a

▼ A map showing the
growth of ancient Rome
from the 300's B.C., when
the Romans began gaining
control of more territory
on the Italian peninsula.
By 272 B.C., they had
conquered most of this
region. Rome's overseas
expansion began with a
series of three wars with
Carthage, a city-state on the
coast of North Africa. By
winning the three Punic
Wars (264–146 B.C.), Rome
gained control of all
Carthaginian territory.

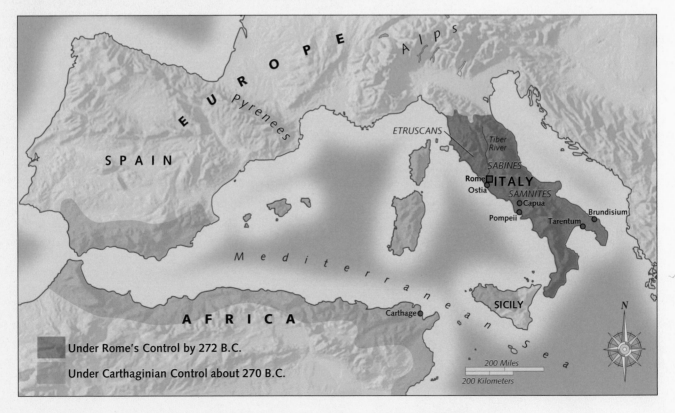

Under Rome's Control by 272 B.C.

Under Carthaginian Control about 270 B.C.

200 Miles

200 Kilometers

succession of kings. The last of these kings was an Etruscan named Tarquin *(TAHR kwihn)* the Proud, who, according to ancient Roman historians, ruled with such harshness that he was overthrown by the Roman **nobles.** Instead of replacing Tarquin with another king, in 509 B.C. the Romans set up a new form of government called a **republic,** with elected leaders called **consuls** *(KON suhlz).*

Roman Expansion

From the earliest years of the Republic, the Romans fought to defend themselves and to extend their territory. After a disastrous attack on Rome around 390 B.C. by the **Gauls** *(gawlz),* who had invaded Italy from the north, the Romans built fortified walls around their city. By 338 B.C., they had gained control of rival communities in Latium, and they extended this control across Etruscan territories in the following century. At the same time, they fought a series of bitter wars against the Samnites, who were eventually defeated in 290 B.C. In 272 B.C., when Roman armies defeated the Greeks in Tarentum *(tuh REHNT uhm),* in southern Italy, Rome ruled most of the Italian peninsula.

▲ A **fresco** *(FREHS koh)* from the 1500's by the Italian artist Jacopo Ripanda *(YAHK oh poh rih PAHN duh).* The fresco depicts the Carthaginian general Hannibal, crossing the Alps seated on one of his war elephants during the Second Punic War.

THE PUNIC WARS

The expansion of Rome brought it into conflict with a rival empire— Carthage in North Africa. Rome and Carthage fought three wars, known as the Punic Wars. *Punici* is the Latin word for "Phoenician" *(fuh NEE shun),* the original settlers of Carthage. Rome eventually defeated Carthage in the Third Punic War in 146 B.C. During the Second Punic War (218-201 B.C.), a Carthaginian *(kahr thuh JIHN ee uhn)* general, Hannibal, crossed the Alps with an army that actually included war elephants, which he had transported from North Africa.

FROM REPUBLIC TO EMPIRE

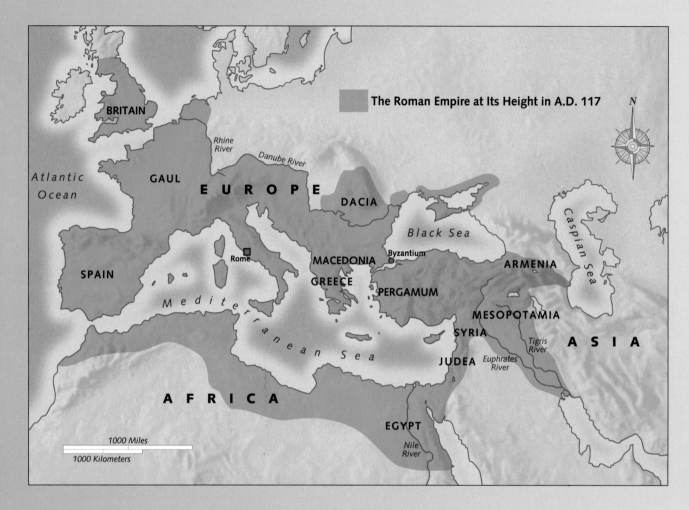

The Roman Empire at Its Height in A.D. 117

After the Second Punic War, Rome began to expand its territories in the eastern Mediterranean. The kingdom of **Macedonia** *(mas uh DOH nee uh)* became a Roman **province** in 146 B.C. In the same year, Roman armies broke up the Achaean *(uh KEE uhn)* League, a **confederation** of 12 Greek cities, and destroyed the league's beautiful capital, Corinth *(KAWR ihnth)*. Roman power extended into Asia when King Attalus *(A tuh luhs)* III of Pergamum *(pehr guh mum)* died without an heir. To avoid a civil war, he left his kingdom to Rome. In 133 B.C., Pergamum (in modern-day Turkey) became a wealthy Roman province.

While Rome formed **alliances** with many of the neighboring **city-states** in Italy, Rome ruled its overseas territories as provinces. Sicily was Rome's first province, acquired in 241 B.C. at the end of the First Punic War. Each province had a Roman governor, whose job was to keep law and order and to oversee the collection of the taxes that provinces had to pay to Rome.

▲ The Roman Empire reached its greatest size under the Emperor Trajan. Before his death in A.D. 117, Trajan conquered Dacia *(DAH chyah),* territory in present-day Romania and Moldova and in parts of Hungary, Bulgaria, and Ukraine. Trajan also expanded Roman territory into western Asia.

The End of the Republic

The Roman **Republic** came to an end in civil war, as Roman generals fought each other for supreme power. In 61 or 60 B.C., three generals—Pompey *(PAHM pee)*, Julius Caesar, and Marcus Licinius Crassus *(MAHR kuhs lih SIHN ee uhs KRAS uhs)*—joined forces to form a powerful if unofficial political alliance known as the First Triumvirate *(try UHM vuhr iht)*. But after the death of Crassus, Pompey became envious of Caesar's military successes in **Gaul**. The power struggle between the two generals ended with Pompey's defeat in Greece in 48 B.C. Pompey fled to Egypt, where he was killed. Caesar led his army into battle and became involved with Egypt's queen, Cleopatra *(klee uh PAT ruh)*, who bore him a child. Caesar took Cleopatra to Rome, where he was assassinated by a group of Roman **nobles** in 44 B.C.

More civil war followed Caesar's death. In 32 B.C., Octavian, Caesar's adopted son, went to war against his former ally, Mark Antony *(AN tuh nee)*, who had been a general in Caesar's army. Antony had the support of Cleopatra. Octavian defeated Antony and Cleopatra's combined fleets in the Battle of Actium *(AK tee uhm)* in 31 B.C. The following year, Egypt became a Roman province. Octavian became the first Roman emperor in 27 B.C. and took the name Augustus, which means "revered one." His reign marked the beginning of a period of stability that lasted until about A.D. 180. This time became known as the Pax Romana *(PAKS roh MAH nuh)*, or Roman Peace. Under Augustus and subsequent emperors, the Roman **Empire** continued to expand, reaching its greatest size under the Emperor Trajan, who ruled from A.D. 98 to 117.

◀ A Roman coin from around the time of Christ shows a member of a **Germanic** *(jur MAN ihk)* tribe—that is, a tribe from regions in modern-day Germany and Britain—handing over a child to the Emperor Augustus. The Romans frequently took hostages from conquered peoples. The hostages served not only as symbols of Roman power and authority, but also as potentially useful tools in diplomatic negotiations.

JULIUS CAESAR (100?–44 B.C.)

Gaius *(GAY uhs)* Julius Caesar was born in Rome to an upper-class family. His military success made him many enemies in Rome. Once he became the Roman **dictator**, Caesar pardoned many of his former opponents and gave them positions of responsibility. But suspicion that Caesar would become a tyrant (an unjust and absolute ruler) and destroy the Republic, remained strong. He was murdered by a group of nobles on March 15 (a date the Romans called the Ides—or middle—of March). To this day, people use the phrase "Beware the Ides of March" as a warning to "take care."

CONSULS AND EMPERORS

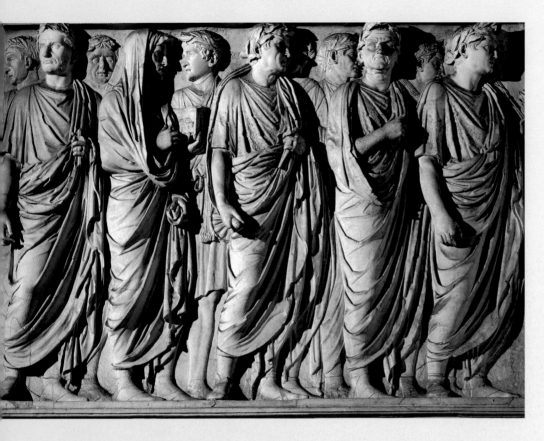

◀ A **relief** sculpture from the north side of a huge marble altar called the Ara Pacis (*AH rah PAH chis;* Altar of Peace) shows senators and priests taking part in a thanksgiving ceremony. The monumental altar was commissioned in 13 B.C. by the Roman Senate to celebrate the period of peace following Augustus's return from victories in Hispania (*hihs PAY nee uh*), present-day Spain and Portugal.

The kings who ruled Rome in the early years of its history were advised by a council called the **Senate.** The Senate was made up of the heads of the leading families in Rome. When the monarchy, or rule by a king, was abolished in 509 B.C., two elected heads of state, called **consuls,** took the place of the king. To prevent any one person from becoming too powerful, the two consuls held office for one year only. The consuls headed the government, and they commanded the army in times of war. They were advised by the members of the Senate, who held office for life.

The Ladder of Offices

A wealthy Roman who wanted to succeed in public life in the 100 years preceding the birth of Christ followed a path called the cursus honorum (*KUR suhs hah NAWR uhm*), a course, or "ladder," of offices. The first step on this course was to serve as a military officer in the army, usually for 10 years. After this, a candidate could run for the office of **magistrate** *(MAJ uh strayt)*, a government post with a one-year term. The most junior post as magistrate was that of quaestor *(KWEHS tuhr)*, one of the officials responsible for Rome's finances. The next step on the ladder was to serve as

▶ A marble head of the Emperor Nero, dating from A.D. 65. Nero was only 16 when he became emperor in A.D. 54 and 30 when he killed himself in A.D. 68. The phrase "to fiddle while Rome burns" is used to describe a person who occupies himself or herself with unimportant matters and neglects priorities during a crisis. It relates to Nero, who was said—probably falsely—to have played a harp while watching Rome burn from the safety of his palace.

ROMAN EMPERORS

Rome was ruled by emperors for around 500 years. Some emperors were successful rulers, but others were extremely unpopular. The behavior of Tiberius's successor, Caligula *(kuh LIHG yuh luh)*—who reigned from A.D. 37 to 41—led many people to believe that he was mad. Caligula was assassinated by the commander of the Praetorian *(pree TAWR ee uhn)* Guard, that is, the soldiers who guarded the emperor. During the reign of another notorious emperor, Nero *(NEER oh)*—who reigned from A.D. 54 to 68—large parts of Rome were destroyed by a disastrous fire. Nero took advantage of the destruction to build a huge and extravagant palace in the burned-out area, which gave support to rumors that he himself had started the fire. Nero's military commanders rebelled against him, and he took his own life in A.D. 68.

an aedile *(EE dyl)*. Aediles had such responsibilities as overseeing public works and weights and measures and organizing some public games. Former aediles might be elected to be a praetor *(PREE tuhr)*. Praetors were judicial officials who were second only to the consuls. If the consuls were absent from Rome, the praetors served in their absence. After serving as a quaestor, magistrates usually entered the Senate. But only after holding the post of praetor could a magistrate stand for election to be a consul.

Imperial Rome

After Augustus took power in 27 B.C., emperors ruled the Roman **Empire.** Augustus continued many traditions of the **Republic,** such as the consuls and the Senate, but as emperor he held supreme authority. The peace and prosperity that flourished during the reign of Augustus inspired many to worship the emperor and, after his death in A.D. 14, he was declared a god. He was succeeded by his adopted son, Tiberius *(ty BEER ee uhs).*

PATRICIANS AND PLEBEIANS

Iⁿ the early days of Rome's history, the wealthiest families had a great deal of power and influence. People from these families were called **patricians** *(puh TRIHSH uhnz)*. People of common birth were known as **plebeians** *(plih BEE uhnz)*. At the beginning of the Roman **Republic,** there was a marked divide between the two classes. In these early times of Rome, only patricians could become government officials or priests. And, until a law was passed in 445 B.C., marriage between patricians and plebeians was forbidden.

The struggle between the patricians, who wanted to protect their power, and the plebeians, who wanted equal rights with the patricians, became known as the Conflict of Orders. The plebeians established their own assembly and elected officials called **tribunes** *(TRIHB yoonz)* to represent them. They forced concessions from the patricians by withdrawing from the city—in effect, going on strike—several times over two centuries. The Conflict of Orders came to an end by 287 B.C., when the plebeians had gained the right to hold public and religious offices. The patricians continued to have significant power, but plebeians who had become wealthy began to join patricians to create a new upper class in Roman society.

▼ A panel from the Domitius Ahenobarbus **Relief** depicts the taking of the census that was held in Rome every five years. The census was taken for tax purposes and for enrolling young men in the Roman army. The marble low relief, dating from around 100 B.C., is believed to have been commissioned by Gnaeus Domitius Ahenobarbus *(NAY us doh MISH uhs uh hen uh BAR buhs)*, who was a **consul** in 122 B.C.

◀ The King's Bath forms part of a spa complex in the town of Bath, in southwest England. It was built, initially in the 1100's, on the foundations of baths constructed by the Romans in the A.D. 100's. The highly complex Roman bath made use of the hot spring water that emerges from the ground at a temperature of 115 °F (46 °C). The Romans named their resort "Aquae Sulis" *(AWK wee SOO liss),* meaning the waters of Sulis, a Roman goddess.

LIVING LIKE A ROMAN

Archaeologists have found from the remains of buildings in places far from Rome that Roman ways of life were adopted by people across the empire. In some parts of the empire, the Romans introduced new luxuries such as grand bathhouses or spacious villas (large homes outside of the cities) with underfloor heating and elaborate **mosaics** *(moh ZAY ihkz).* Such luxuries helped to encourage local leaders to be eager and proud to be part of Rome's Empire.

Citizens and Noncitizens

For much of Rome's history, the Romans made a distinction between people who were residents of the city of Rome, known as **citizens**, and people from the territories that were allied to or conquered by Rome, known as noncitizens. Both citizens and noncitizens were free, unlike slaves, who were treated as property. Citizens, however, had rights and privileges under Roman law that did not apply to noncitizens. Only citizens could become government officials. Citizens included people from all social classes: patricians; **equites** *(EHK wuh teez),* rich men who originally served in the army as cavalrymen, but later came close to senators in their social standing; and plebeians.

As Rome expanded, it granted citizenship to people in other territories. The **Sabines,** for example, became full Roman citizens in 268 B.C. And in A.D. 212, under the Emperor Caracalla *(kar uh KAL uh),* citizenship was extended to all free inhabitants of the Roman **Empire,** that is, everyone except slaves. Citizenship applied to men, women, and children alike, though women and children were not permitted to vote. The privileges of citizenship helped to promote loyalty across the Roman territories.

THE ARMY

In the early years of Roman expansion, Roman **citizens** were called up to serve in the army as the need arose. Once a military campaign was completed, the men returned to their homes and their previous jobs. Many soldiers served for several campaigns in succession, though most returned home after a year or two. During the **Republic,** Rome's armies also included many noncitizen soldiers, called **auxiliaries** *(awg ZIHL yuhr eez).* These forces were drawn from territories that were allied to Rome and were bound by treaty to provide troops for Rome's wars. Only during the reign of Augustus did the army become a permanent salaried career for its soldiers. The normal length of service in the imperial army was between 16 and 28 years.

▼ A scene from the movie *Ben Hur* shows actors dressed as Roman soldiers.

TRAJAN'S COLUMN

After the death in A.D. 117 of Emperor Trajan, a **column** was erected in Rome to commemorate his military victories. The column is entirely carved in **relief** scenes depicting Trajan's campaigns in Dacia, part of which is in present-day Romania. These scenes show all aspects of the life of a Roman soldier on the march—building camps and forts, crossing rivers, listening to Trajan himself, fighting battles. The scenes provide valuable evidence of how the Roman army operated.

Trajan's Column, which is 98 feet (30 meters) tall, still stands today in Trajan's **Forum** in Rome. The inside of the column is hollow, with stairs that allow access to a viewing platform at the top. It is said that Trajan's ashes were placed inside the column, but there is no evidence that it was intended as his tomb.

The **legion** formed the backbone of the army. Each legion was made up of about 5,000 foot soldiers, or legionaries *(LEE juh NEHR eez)*, all of them Roman citizens. Auxiliary soldiers usually had such specialized skills as fighting with slings, with bows and arrows, or on horseback. By the early A.D. 100's, all auxiliary troops (and their families) were granted Roman citizenship when they retired from the army. The Praetorian Guard, established in the reign of Augustus, acted as a bodyguard for the emperor and was the only group of soldiers stationed in the city of Rome.

Weapons, Armor, and Tactics

The legionaries were well-trained and disciplined soldiers. A legionary in the imperial army wore armor to cover his chest, stomach, and shoulders. There were several types of armor, including chain mail (tiny rings of metal linked together) and armor made from thin iron strips that were held together on the inside with leather straps. Around his waist, a legionary wore a belt from which dangled leather strips studded with metal. These strips may have offered some protection for the groin—they also made a fearsome jangling noise as the legionaries marched, which possibly helped to intimidate an enemy. A legionary carried a shield, two javelins with iron heads for throwing, and a short sword. Legions often marched great distances, carrying with them everything they needed to survive, including tools for digging (to make camp at night), cooking pots, clothes, and rations (the food issued to each soldier). On their feet, legionaries wore special military leather sandals that had nails driven into the soles to help them withstand the miles of marching.

WOMEN

▶ A **relief** sculpture dating from the first century after the birth of Christ depicts a woman apothecary *(uh POTH uh KEHR ee),* a person who prepares and sells medicines. Behind her, an assistant grinds up an ingredient to be used in a cure.

Men dominated public life in Rome; there were no women generals, senators, or **consuls.** Women were considered to be unfit for military service or public speaking. Nevertheless, some high-ranking women, such as wives of senators or the wife or mother of the emperor, gained great influence. The wife of the Emperor Augustus, Livia Drusilla *(LIHV ee uh droo SIHL uh),* who lived from 58 B.C. to A.D. 29, advised her husband on imperial matters and was ruthless in her determination to secure the throne for Tiberius, her son from an earlier marriage.

Women's Work

Women were mainly expected to be wives and mothers and to look after the household. During the **Republic,** a woman became her husband's property when she married. By the end of the Republic, however, this practice had ended, and a married woman usually kept both her legal rights and any property she had owned before her marriage.

Domestic duties included running the household, looking after the children, and spinning and weaving to make clothes for the family. Some women, mainly of the lower classes, had jobs outside the home. Women worked as midwives, shopkeepers and market traders, and craftworkers; some women worked in agriculture. There were also many female slaves.

Vestal Virgins

Vesta, the goddess of the household, had an important place in Roman life. Vesta's symbol was the fire in the hearth *(hahrth)*—the stone or brick floor of a fireplace—and every home had a shrine that honored her. Vesta was also the protector of the city of Rome, and her temple was the only one served by priestesses rather than a priest. The Romans considered it a great honor to be chosen as one of these six priestesses, known as Vestal Virgins. The Vestal Virgins often had considerable power and influence in Roman political life. They were required to serve for 30 years, however, during which time they had to remain unmarried.

JULIA AGRIPPINA (A.D. 15 TO 59)

Julia Agrippina *(AG ruh PY nuh)* was one of the most influential women in imperial Rome. She was a sister of the Emperor Caligula. She married her uncle, the Emperor Claudius, in A.D. 49 and was the mother of Claudius's successor, Nero (who was her son from a previous marriage). It was widely believed in Rome that Agrippina poisoned Claudius to free the throne for her 16-year-old son. She was a powerful figure in the first year of Nero's reign, but as Nero grew in confidence, he came to resent his mother's power. On his orders, she was murdered at her country home in A.D. 59. Her image appears on the **bronze** coin (above) made in A.D. 56, three years before her death.

FARMERS

▲ A Roman stone pillar dating from the A.D. 100's from Gaul (present-day France) depicts farmers at work turning the soil (bottom) and selling their produce at a market (top).

The early Romans were shepherds and farmers. Even when the **empire** was at its height at around A.D. 100, at least 85 percent of the population still worked and lived on the land. Rome relied on the agricultural produce grown by its farmers to feed its armies and the populations of its cities. In the early **Republic,** many farmers owned their own small farms, but as soldier-farmers were required to spend long periods away from home, and as wealth and slaves began to flood in as a result of victories in the Punic Wars, many small farms were taken over by larger landowners. Some large estates, called latifundia *(LAT uh FUHN dee uh)*, were worked by teams of slaves; others had tenant farmers. The owners of such estates lived in large country houses called villas. Ordinary people lived in simple houses made of sun-dried bricks.

Farm Work

Roman farmers grew crops that flourished in the hot Mediterranean climate. Cereal crops included emmer (an ancient variety of wheat), barley, oats, rye, and millet. The cultivation of olives (mainly for oil) and of grapes (mainly for wine) was also extremely important. Cattle, sheep, and goats were raised for their meat and milk and also for their hides, which was tanned into leather.

Farm work was back-breaking labor, but with a plentiful supply of slaves, the Romans had little incentive to develop labor-saving farm implements. Roman farmworkers used such tools as spades, sickles, and scythes (*sythz*—curved blades used for reaping) to work the soil and tend crops. Pitchforks were used to move hay that was fed to livestock. The Romans did, however, adopt some of the agricultural machines that they learned about as they acquired territories. The wheeled plough originally came from **Gaul**, and the wheeled threshing machine (used to thresh, or separate, kernels of grain from stalks) probably came from Carthage.

VINES

Wine was very important in Roman life. There were no tea, coffee, or chocolate drinks, and though beer was known, drinking beer was not common. The Romans grew grapes in Italy for the production of wine, and they imported wine from other parts of their empire, such as Greece, Spain, Gaul, and North Africa. Grape vines needed careful attention. They had to be pruned and supported to keep the grapes off the ground. At harvest time, the grapes were picked by hand, then stepped on to crush the fruit and extract the juice for the wine. The Roman writer Columella *(kohl yoo MEHL uh)*, who wrote sometime during the first 100 years after Christ's birth, gave detailed information about the cultivation of grapevines in his work *Scriptores de Re Rustica (skrihp TAWR ees duh ray RUHS tih kuh)*, or *Writings on Country Matters.*

◀ Workers tend a vineyard in North Africa during the winter, in a **mosaic** dating from around A.D. 200. Raising grapes was labor-intensive, but wine was an important drink throughout the Roman Empire.

SLAVES AND FREED SLAVES

Under Roman law, slaves were considered to be the property of their owners. Most slaves were captured in wars and then brought back to the Roman **Empire.** Some slaves were brought in from lands outside the empire by traders or were captured and then sold by Mediterranean pirates. A child born to a slave mother in ancient Rome was also automatically regarded as a slave. If that child's father was freeborn, he could free the child when he or she turned 16. The child born of a slave father and a free mother was considered to be freeborn.

▼ A marble **relief** dating from the A.D. 100's to 200's from Miletus *(MIHL uh tus),* in present-day Turkey. The sculpture depicts three prisoners of war chained at the neck and being led by a Roman captor. Such prisoners were often sold into slavery locally or taken back to Rome as slaves.

Slavery was vital to the economy of the Roman world; it is estimated that in the first 100 years after Christ's birth, slaves made up about one-third of the population in Italy. Slaves were sold at markets. One such market, on the Greek island of Delos *(dehl ohs)* in the Aegean *(ee JEE uhn)* Sea, could process up to 10,000 slaves a day.

Conditions for slaves varied greatly. Household slaves were often treated well, and some came to be regarded as members of the family by their owners. However, slaves who worked on the land, in mines, or as oarsmen on Roman galleys often endured terrible conditions. Many thousands of

Spartacus (? – 71 B.C.)

Spartacus *(SPAHR tuh kuhs)* was born in Thrace *(thrays)*, a region northeast of Greece in the Balkan Peninsula. He served in the Roman army, then deserted and was captured and sold as a slave. He was trained as a **gladiator** *(GLAD ee AY tuhr)*—a warrior who fought bloody battles with other gladiators or wild beasts to entertain spectators. In 73 B.C., Spartacus and other gladiators escaped from their masters in the town of Capua *(KAP yoo wuh)* in southern Italy and took refuge on Mount Vesuvius *(vuh SOO vee uhs)*. They were soon joined by thousands of other runaway slaves. Led by Spartacus, this army of slaves took control of much of southern Italy. Spartacus's rebel army was eventually defeated by Roman forces in 71 B.C., and Spartacus himself was killed during the fighting.

slaves met early death in the mines of the Roman Empire. It was almost certain death to become a slave oarsman on one of the Roman galleys, the ships that sailed the Mediterranean.

Freedom

Slaves could buy or be given their freedom. Many owners paid their slaves as an incentive to make them work hard. By saving enough money, slaves could gain **manumission** *(MAN yuh MIHSH uhn)*— the formal release from slavery made by an owner. Some owners chose to free their slaves, either because they could not work any more or as a reward for good service. Sometimes, a slave was freed so that her owner was permitted to marry her. Freed slaves, known as freedmen or freedwomen, sometimes continued to work for their former masters. A freed slave could not hold public office, but his or her children could become **magistrates** and even move on to higher office from there. One striking and unusual example of such social mobility is Pertinax *(PUR tuhn aks)*, the son of a freed slave, who was briefly emperor in 193 B.C.

◀ A **mosaic** of a slave serving a Roman wine from a pottery jar known as an amphora *(AM fuhr uh)*. Owners and their domestic slaves usually lived at close quarters in the household, and strong friendships sometimes developed between master and slave.

LAW, CRIME, AND PUNISHMENT

◀ The ruins of the law court in the Forum in Pompeii *(pom PAY)*. Only the bases remain of the **columns** that once supported the building's central court. The city of Pompeii, near present-day Naples, Italy, was buried in volcanic ash when nearby Mount Vesuvius erupted in A.D. 79.

The Romans established their first written law code in 450 B.C. This code, known as the Law of the Twelve Tables, grew out of the ongoing struggle between the **patricians** and the **plebeians** (see pages 12-13). Before this time, only patricians could interpret the law, which was based on unwritten custom. The plebeians distrusted this practice and, beginning in 450 B.C., a council of 10 men drew up and inscribed 12 laws onto tablets that were displayed in the Roman **Forum** (the place where trials occurred). These laws were based on earlier criminal and **civil law**, as well as on religious customs.

As Rome grew, its legal system developed and became more complex than the Law of the Twelve Tables. The ancient Romans were the first people to have lawyers—professional experts whose job was to interpret the law on behalf of others. The Romans

CRIMINAL ENTERTAINMENT

Slaves who were found guilty of a crime and certain other people, such as Christians, were generally executed in public in horrible ways. Christians and some condemned slaves were used as popular entertainment when they were thrown unarmed into the arena of an **amphitheater** to face wild animals. Without any means of defense, they were torn to pieces. They were also put to death by crucifixion—being nailed and tied to a cross made of wood. After the slave revolt of 73 to 71 B.C. that was led by a **gladiator,** Spartacus, 6,000 slaves were crucified along the Appian *(AP ee uhn)* Way (the main road into Rome from the south).

developed the jus civile *(juhs sih VY lee)*, or civil law, which applied to Roman **citizens** only. As the Roman world expanded, the jus gentium *(juhs JEHN tee uhm)*, or law of nations, developed. This law applied to citizens and noncitizens alike. The law was enforced by **magistrates** and by the governors of Rome's foreign territories. In the A.D. 500's, the Emperor Justinian *(juhs TIHN ee uhn)* I of the East Roman **Empire** reorganized Roman law, and the law books written in his time provide much of our knowledge about the Roman legal system.

Crime and Punishment

In Roman society, the status of an offender played a large part in deciding what punishment he or she should suffer. Punishments for slaves were far harsher than those inflicted on free men and women. For a Roman citizen, the removal of the rights attached to citizenship was considered a

fitting punishment for many crimes. In many cases, citizens who were accused of a capital offense (a crime punishable by death), such as murder or treason, could choose to go into exile rather than face execution; the exiled person lost all of his or her property and could never return to Roman-controlled territory. If an upper-class Roman citizen did face the death penalty, he or she was usually beheaded in private (the term *capital punishment* comes from caput *[KAY puht]*, the **Latin** word for "head"). Less important people were executed in public. The Romans did not use prison as a form of long-term punishment, though they did have small prisons for the short-term imprisonment of offenders and for convicted criminals awaiting execution.

▼ A Roman amphitheater in present-day Tarragona *(TAR uh GOH nuh)*, Spain, was the site of the execution of that city's Christian bishop and his followers in A.D. 259. Christianity was outlawed in the Roman Empire until A.D. 337.

BELIEFS AND GODS

The Romans believed in many gods and goddesses. These **deities** *(DEE uh teez)* were thought to watch over all aspects of life, from the hearth and the home to war and hunting. The Romans held ceremonies to worship and make offerings to their gods; in return they hoped for practical help with everyday matters. Before battles, for example, Roman soldiers sacrificed animals to the gods, hoping to ensure a favorable outcome. From the time of Augustus, many emperors were worshiped as gods after their deaths.

The Capitoline Triad

Many of the Roman gods and goddesses had long been worshiped on the Italian peninsula. The sky god Jupiter was worshiped throughout the region on the summits of hills. He became the special protector of Rome and the Romans' chief god. Like many other Roman gods and goddesses, he also became identified with his Greek equivalent, Zeus *(zoos)*. The Romans became familiar with the Greek gods as they began the conquest of Greece in the 100's B.C. Eventually, the traits of the gods of Greece and Rome were often fused (joined together).

The main center for the worship of Jupiter in ancient Rome was a magnificent temple on the Capitoline Hill. This hill also housed shrines to Juno *(JOO noh)*, the goddess of women and childbirth, and to Minerva *(muh NUR vuh)*, the goddess of handicrafts and wisdom. Juno was the sister and wife of Jupiter, and she was identified with the Greek goddess Hera *(HIHR uh)*, the wife of Zeus. Minerva was closely associated with the Greek goddess of war and wisdom, Athena *(uh THEE nuh)*. The three deities—Jupiter, Juno, and Minerva—were known as the Capitoline triad *(TRY ad)*.

▲ A plaque from the Temple of Apollo that once stood on the Palatine Hill in Rome shows Apollo (left) with his twin sister, Artemis. Apollo was a Greek god, but the Romans also worshiped him as the god of healing and prophecy. The emperor Augustus claimed Apollo as his protector, and the temple was built next to Augustus's house on the Palatine.

The Romans had gods and goddesses to watch over all sorts of everyday items and events. Janus *(JAY nuhs)* was an important Roman god who had no Greek equivalent. He was depicted with two faces that looked in opposite directions. One of his functions was as the god of doorways, keeping watch over both comings and goings. Other important household gods were the Lares *(LAR eez),* thought to be the spirits of ancestors, and the Penates *(puh NAY teez),* thought to protect household supplies.

Other Gods and Goddesses

As the god of war, Mars was a very important deity for the Romans. He was also considered to be the father of Romulus and Remus, the **legendary** founders of Rome. Mars was originally a god of farmland and fertility, but he became the god of war after being associated with the Greek war god Ares *(AIR eez).* Similarly, the Roman goddess of the moon, Diana, was identified with the Greek goddess of hunting and wild animals, Artemis *(AHR tuh mihs),* and took on her characteristics. The Romans also adopted gods and goddesses from more far-flung places. A cult associated with the **Persian** god of light, Mithra *(MIHTH ruh),* became popular among Roman soldiers across the **empire,** and worship of the Egyptian goddess Isis *(EYE sihs)* also became widespread.

▶ A shrine to the household gods found in a home excavated in Pompeii. In the center is the "genius," the spirit of the head of the family, dressed in a toga, with his head covered. He carries a dish for offerings in his right hand and, in his left hand, a box of incense *(IHN sehns),* a substance that gives off a sweet smell when burned. On either side of the genius are the Lares, both holding drinking horns and wine buckets.

PRIESTS AND CEREMONIES

The government of Rome controlled public religious practices and ceremonies. Most priests were government officials who were elected or appointed and who held the office of priest as one of their many duties. They were required to perform ceremonies and sacrifices in the belief that this would gain the favor of the gods. Apart from the Vestal Virgins (see page 17), priests were usually men. By the end of the **Republic,** there were four main groups of priests, called colleges. The most important college was that of the pontiffs *(PON tihfz)*, who controlled (among other things) ceremonies, sacrifices, games and festivals, and religious law. The supreme priest was the pontifex maximus *(PON tuh fehks MAK suh muhs)*. During the **empire,** this position was held by the emperor.

Priests known as augurs *(AW guhrz)* made up another of the colleges. The augurs were concerned with **divination**—the practice of telling the future and trying to understand the will of the gods. The augurs mainly observed the movements of birds to look for what they believed were signs from the gods. Other natural occurrences, such as an earthquake or an eclipse, could also be interpreted as signs, called portents *(PAWR tehntz)*.

A third college of priests, the Priesthood of 15, guarded the **Sibylline** *(SIHB uh leen)* **Books.** Members of the fourth college, the Seven Feasters, were responsible for the feasts held at festivals.

▶ A **relief** from the A.D. 100's from the Church of Saint Luca and Saint Martina in Rome depicts the Emperor Marcus Aurelius *(MAHR kuhs aw REE lee uhs)* leading a sacrifice before the Temple of Jupiter in Rome. This great temple on the Capitoline Hill was the largest and most important in Rome. It was built of marble, and the interior was richly decorated. The doors were plated with gold.

A NEW RELIGION

In the first 100 years after Christ's birth, a new religion, Christianity, began to spread across the Roman world. Many people turned to this new religion, but the Roman authorities saw Christianity as a threat. Christians refused to make sacrifices to the Roman gods and goddesses, and as a result, they were persecuted and often put to death by the Romans. However, under the Emperor Constantine, Christianity became the main religion of the empire after A.D. 337.

Temples and Sacrifices

A Roman temple was considered to be the home of the god or goddess to whom it was dedicated. An image of the god was often kept inside the temple. People who came to worship at the temple usually gathered outside the building to pray and make their offerings to the **deity.** Animal sacrifice was a very important part of Roman religion. Sacrifices were made for many reasons—for example, as part of the ceremonies associated with religious festivals or to give thanks to the gods for a specific event. The inner organs of the sacrificed animal were burned and offered to the gods. The rest of the meat was cooked and eaten as part of a sacrificial banquet.

▶ A **fresco** from Pompeii shows a man leading a bull about to be sacrificed. Animals considered suitable for sacrifice included pigs, sheep, goats, and cattle.

THE ROMAN CALENDAR

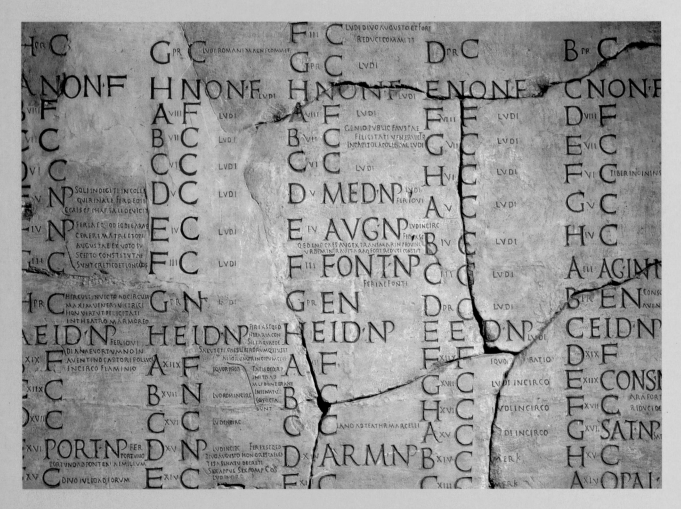

The Romans established the basis of the calendar and the names of the days and months that much of the world uses today. The early calendar used by the Romans had only 10 months and did not match up with the solar year (the time in which Earth travels once around the sun). The 10 months were named Martius *(MAHR tee uhs)*, Aprilis *(AH prih lihs)*, Maius *(MY yoos)*, Junius *(YOO nee uhs)*, Quintilis *(KWIHN tih lihs)*, Sextilis *(SEHKS tih lihs)*, September, October, November, and December. The last six names were taken from the **Latin** words for 5, 6, 7, 8, 9, and 10. The Roman year began in March (Martius), named after the god Mars.

The Julian Calendar

An early Roman king, Numa Pompilius *(NYOO muh pahm PIHL ee uhs)*, is said to have added January and February to the calendar. January, which later became the first month of the year, was named after Janus, the two-faced god of ends and beginnings. The Latin word *februare* means "to

▲ A fragment of a **fresco** showing a Roman calendar from the period just before Julius Caesar's calendar reforms. The days are noted by a letter and a Roman numeral. The days also have letters to show whether they are fasti (F) or nefasti (N). NP stands for nefasti publici—days of great public festivals—while C marks the days when comitia (assemblies) could meet.

▼ A marble bust of Julius Caesar, the general and statesman responsible for reordering the Roman calendar. According to an account by the biographer Plutarch (*PLOO tahrk;* A.D. 46?–120?), Caesar "put the problem before the best scholars and mathematicians of the day" to solve the confusion created by the old Roman calendar.

purify," and February was a month of purification before the new year. The addition of January and February made the Roman year 355 days long. Under this system, in every other year the chief priest added an extra month to make the Roman calendar correspond to the solar year. This was an imprecise system, and by the time of Julius Caesar, the Roman calendar differed by about three months from the seasons.

Julius Caesar ordered the calendar to be revised and declared that 46 B.C. should have 445 days to start the new calendar at the right time. Romans called this time the year of confusion. From 45 B.C., the Julian calendar divided the year into 12 months, each month with 30 or 31 days except February, which had 29 days. Every four years, February had 30 days.

The Romans renamed Quintilis after Julius Caesar, leading to the present name July, and renamed Sextilis to honor the Emperor Augustus (August). The Roman **Senate** also moved a day from February to August to make it 31 days—the same as July—leaving February with 28 or 29 days, as it is today.

ROMAN ARCHITECTURE

The Romans were skilled builders, and many of their theaters, temples, baths, bridges, and roads have survived to this day. The people who lived in the territories of the Roman **Empire** all had their own building traditions with different styles. The Romans themselves, however, were greatly influenced by the styles of Greek architecture, though they adapted and further developed these styles. For example, the Romans based the design of their temples on those of the Greeks, with a sloping roof over a triangular **pediment** *(PEHD uh muhnt)* that was supported by decorative **columns**.

The Romans built a great variety of structures. Besides temples, palaces, and houses, they built public baths, huge **amphitheaters** and arenas for public spectacles and games, **aqueducts** *(AK wuh duhktz)* for transporting water over long distances, and thousands of miles of roads that connected all the territories of their vast empire.

▼ Almost 2,000 years old, the Pantheon, a temple to all the Roman gods, still stands in the center of Rome. Because it was turned into a Christian church, it was never plundered for building materials like most other ancient structures in Rome.

THE PANTHEON

The Pantheon is a circular structure built as a temple in Rome. The brick-and-concrete structure was completed under the rule of the Emperor Hadrian *(HAY dree uhn)* in about A.D. 126. Hadrian dedicated the temple to all the Roman gods. The roof is a concrete dome that rises about 142 feet (43 meters) from the floor at its highest point. The center of the dome has a circular opening (30 feet, or 9 meters, in diameter), called an oculus *(AHK ya lus)*, which floods the interior with light. The builders of the Pantheon used a type of extremely lightweight rock, called pumice, as the rubble for the concrete to reduce the weight toward the top of the dome. The Pantheon still stands in the center of Rome, the best preserved of any ancient Roman building. The dome is the oldest in existence.

Building Breakthroughs

The Romans used the types of stone found close to Rome for their buildings, particularly a volcanic rock called tuff and a type of limestone called travertine *(TRAV uhr teen)*. They also used marble, often to decorate their buildings.

Houses were usually built with bricks, which were mass-produced in huge quantities. However, it was the invention of concrete that allowed Roman builders to construct some of their most spectacular structures, such as the Pantheon *(PAN thee on)*.

The Romans made concrete with a fine volcanic ash called pozzuolana *(POT swoh LAH nuh)*, which was mixed with lime (calcium oxide) and water to create cement—a cement that would set even under water. Into this cement they added stone rubble for concrete that was both extremely strong and waterproof. Concrete walls were generally covered (faced) with another material, usually stone or tile.

ENGINEERING AND SCIENCE

◀ The Pont du Gard in southern France is a remarkable feat of Roman engineering. The structure's overall height is 161 feet (49 meters), making it the tallest aqueduct ever built by the ancient Romans. The first (or lowest) tier is made up of 6 arches and has a road on it; the second tier has 11 arches; and the third tier, which actually carries the water, has 47 arches.

The invention of concrete coincided with Roman experiments with arches. From the simple arch, the Romans developed the dome and the **vault**—a row of arches joined together in the form of a tunnel to create what is known as a barrel vault. These two breakthroughs in Roman engineering—concrete and the use of the arch—allowed the Romans to build large structures. In the Colosseum in Rome, for example, concrete arched vaults supported the great weight of the tiers of spectator seating around the central arena.

Aqueducts

The Romans used their engineering skills to build spectacular bridges and **aqueducts**. A clean water supply was vital for the population of Rome, and much of the city's water had to come from the surrounding countryside, some from as far as 57 miles (92 kilometers) away. The water was moved through paved ditches, lead pipes, and along arched aqueducts. Grand projects such as the public baths that were built during the **empire**

ON THE WATERS OF THE CITY OF ROME

A great deal about Roman engineering is known from studying ruins and other archaeological evidence. Detailed descriptions in texts written by Roman authors survive. One of these texts, *On the Waters of the City of Rome*, was written by Sextus Julius Frontinus (*SEHKS tuhs JOO lee uhs FRAHN tih nuhs;* A.D. 35 to around 103), who was superintendent of aqueducts under the Emperor Nerva:

"As a rule, those parts of the aqueducts which are carried on arches or … the parts that cross rivers suffer most from the effects of age or of violent storms. These, therefore, must be put in order with care and dispatch. The underground portions, not being subjected to either heat or frost, are less liable to injury…."

required vast amounts of water, and several aqueducts are named after the emperors who ordered their construction. The Romans built aqueducts throughout their empire. Probably the most famous Roman bridge and aqueduct that is still standing today is in southern France. The Pont du Gard *(POHN doo GAHRD)*, or Bridge of the Gard, was part of a 30-mile- (50-kilometer-) long aqueduct that carried water over the Gard River to the Roman town that today is Nimes *(neem)*, France.

Scientists

As Roman power and influence spread, interest in the world that was opening up around them grew. Many Greek scientists flourished under Roman rule. For example, Strabo *(STRAY boh*—63 B.C.? to A.D. 24?) was a Greek geographer and historian who studied and lived in Rome for many years. His 17-volume *Geography* described all parts of the known world at that time. The astronomer and geographer Ptolemy *(TOL uh mee*—A.D. 100? to 165?) was also of Greek ancestry. Ptolemy set out the theory that the moon, sun, planets, and stars all move around Earth. This view was accepted throughout Europe until the 1500's.

◀ An engraving made in the 1600's of the Roman writer and scientist Pliny the Elder, who lived from A.D. 23 or 24 to 79. His 37-volume work, *Natural History,* is used by historians today to learn about scientific understanding in Pliny's time.

THE BUILDINGS OF ANCIENT ROME

Ancient Rome was the center of the Roman **Empire,** and by the first 100 years after Christ's birth it had a population of about 1 million people. The city was full of magnificent public buildings, many of which can still be seen as impressive ruins in modern-day Rome.

The Forum

The **Forum** was the area of Rome that served as the government and legal center of both the **Republic** and the empire. Buildings in the Forum included the Curia *(KYUR ee uh)*, where the **Senate** met; the law courts; and several important temples, including those dedicated to Saturn (a god of fertility and planting) and Concord (a god who could bring harmonious agreement). The Tabularium *(tab yoo LAIR ee uhm)* held a vast quantity of official documents, including treaties, legal papers, and records of election results. The ground on which the Forum stood was originally marshland that was drained by the Cloaca Maxima *(klo AY kuh MAK sih muh)*, or Great Drain, one of the world's earliest sewage systems. Originally a stream, the course followed by the Cloaca Maxima was paved by the Romans and was used to carry sewer water away from the city and into the Tiber River.

▼ The ruins of the Roman Forum. On the left are the remains of the Temple of Saturn, the oldest temple in the Forum, dating from the 400's B.C. The three **columns** in the distance at right are from the Temple of Castor *(KAS tuhr)* and Pollux *(POL uhks)*.

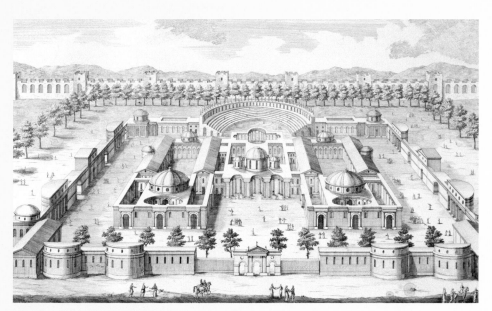

◀ A 1721 engraving presents an imagined reconstruction of the Baths of Diocletian. It gives a good idea of the immense size of these grand public baths, the largest in Rome. The main bath buildings covered 27 acres (11 hectares).

FIRE HAZARD

Rome's wealthy inhabitants lived on its hills, where the air tended to be fresher. The emperor had a huge palace on the Palatine Hill. Ordinary people, however, lived in tall **tenement** *(TEHN uh muhnt)* buildings—five to six stories high—that lined the narrow streets—some as narrow as 10 feet (3 meters) across. The bottoms of these buildings were stone or brick. The top floors, however, were usually made of wood. Fire was a constant hazard, particularly since people used oil lamps for light and used fires in open braziers *(BRAY zhuhrs)*, or large metal trays, for cooking and for heat. In A.D. 6, Augustus began a fire department, known as the Vigiles *(VIH jih lehs)*, after an unusually terrible fire in the city of Rome. The Vigiles (meaning "watchers") patrolled the city of Rome, looking for fires and acting as police as well. Each unit had its own fire engine (a large water pump on a wagon) that was pulled by horses. Once the Vigiles located a source of water near a fire, they would place the pump in the water and begin moving water toward the fire using a bucket brigade (a line of people passing buckets).

Baths and Entertainment

Ancient Rome had several public bathhouses that were highly luxurious places for relaxing and meeting friends. The biggest were those of the emperors Caracalla, built in the A.D. 200's, and Diocletian *(DY uh KLEE shuhn)*, built in the A.D. 300's. The Baths of Diocletian were the largest in Rome, serving up to 3,000 people at a time. The bath buildings had pools for swimming, areas for exercising or playing games, both warm and cold baths, and steam rooms. There were separate areas for men and for women.

For more excitement, Romans watched blood-thirsty spectacles at the Colosseum, also called the **Flavian Amphitheater,** or chariot racing at the Circus Maximus *(SUR kuhs MAK suh muhs)*. Construction of the Colosseum was started during the reign of the Emperor Vespasian *(veh SPAY zhee uhn)*, who ruled from A.D. 69 to 79. The Colosseum, named for a nearby colossal *(kuh LOS uhl;* very large) statue, is oval in shape and held up to 50,000 spectators. It could even be flooded to accommodate mock naval battles with real Roman ships. The Circus Maximus was also amazing—it held around 250,000 people. Christians were put to death for the enjoyment of the mob in both the Colosseum and the Circus Maximus.

PAINTINGS, MOSAICS, AND SCULPTURES

The Romans were great lovers of art. Roman sculptors and painters borrowed styles from the **Etruscans** and the Greeks, among others.

Sculpture

Following the traditions of the Etruscans, many early Roman sculptors worked in **bronze** or **terra cotta**. Statues made from terra cotta were usually brightly painted and were often used to decorate temple roofs. After the Romans conquered Greece and territories in the eastern Mediterranean, huge numbers of paintings and sculptures were brought back to Rome as spoils of war. Many Greek artists also traveled to Rome to work.

The materials and styles used by Greek sculptors were adopted by the Romans, and many Roman sculptures were copies of earlier Greek ones. Roman statues and busts, usually done in marble, often showed recognizable individuals, with facial features and hair carved in great detail. The Romans also used sculpture to record and celebrate notable events. Scenes were carved in **relief** (with the design projecting from a flat background) onto public buildings and such monuments as triumphal arches and **columns.**

◀ The bronze statue of the emperor Marcus Aurelius was probably made just after the emperor's death in A.D. 180. It is twice life-size and was originally gilded (covered in a thin layer of gold) to give the impression of solid gold. The emperor is portrayed in a military **tunic** (*TOO nihk*) and cloak, with his right arm outstretched. The statue is displayed at the Capitoline Museum in Rome.

Walls and Floors

The Romans brought back paintings on panels from Greece, but painting directly onto walls, or **fresco** painting, became very fashionable during the period of the **empire.** The houses of the wealthy were decorated with scenes from Greek and Roman **mythology,** from history, and from everyday life. Just as with sculpture, Roman paintings were often very realistic.

Creating **mosaics** was a Roman specialty used to decorate floors (and sometimes walls and ceilings too). A mosaic is made by pressing small pieces of colored glass or stone into a soft mortar. The pieces, called tesserae *(TEHS uh ree)*, fit together to form a picture or pattern. The Romans learned this technique from the Greeks and then spread it throughout their empire.

THE PAINTINGS AND MOSAICS OF POMPEII

The best-preserved Roman wall paintings and mosaics are at Pompeii, a Roman port that was buried by Mount Vesuvius in A.D. 79. The art at this site was preserved by the volcanic ash and stone that covered Pompeii for nearly 1,700 years before its accidental rediscovery in 1748. The gradual excavation of Pompeii over the past 250 years has revealed fine mosaics and colorful frescoes, such as the painting below from the so-called Villa of Mysteries.

METAL, GLASS, AND POTTERY

The remaining examples of Roman work in what is usually considered fine art—painting and sculpture—are some of the best in the world. The items made by the **artisans** of Rome, however, were also innovative and beautifully crafted and represent some of the finest examples of their kind in the ancient world.

Metalwork

Rome's vast **empire** provided ample raw materials for its highly skilled artisans. Gold, silver, copper, and other metals were mined in Spain, and Italy itself had rich deposits of iron. Britain also had iron, lead, and tin. The latter was used to produce **bronze,** a highly useful mixture of copper and tin. Metalworkers used iron to make weapons and armor; lead for water pipes in Roman plumbing; and gold and silver for fine jewelry and tableware.

Glasswork

The manufacture of glass was developed into an art during Roman times. In the 100 years preceding the birth of Christ, someone along the eastern Mediterranean coast discovered that glass could be worked by blowing through a tube into a bulb of molten (melted) glass to create a hollow shape. This technique allowed glass objects to be manufactured quickly and cheaply. When this region became part of the Roman world, artisans who traveled to Rome brought the technique with them. Many Roman glass containers were made by blowing the glass into decorative molds, after which the molds were removed.

▲ A silver bucket found in the House of Menander at Pompeii. The bucket is decorated with **relief** work of the goddess Venus bathing while attended by her maids.

Glassmaking became an important craft in Italy in the 100 years after the birth of Christ, and it spread to other parts of the Roman Empire, notably the valleys of the Rhone *(rohn)* River in France and Rhine *(reyn)* River in Germany. The Romans used glass to make a wide variety of objects—beads, small bottles for cosmetics and perfumes, window panes, and **mosaics.** Merchants also used glass jars and bottles to pack and transport oil, wine, and other foodstuffs across the Mediterranean Sea.

Pottery

By the time of Augustus, there were large-scale pottery industries based around the town of Arretium *(ahr RAY tee uhm)*—modern-day Arezzo *(ah REHT tsoh)*—in Italy, and in **Gaul,** near present-day Lyon *(lyawn)* in France. The shiny, red pottery decorated with raised designs that was produced at these workshops became extremely popular. During the first 100 years after the birth of Christ, artisans in Roman **provinces** in North Africa began to make imitations of this red pottery, which were sold throughout the Mediterranean. This African pottery—mostly such tableware as plates, cups, and bowls—also became highly popular in the empire and beyond.

THE PORTLAND VASE

The Portland vase is a famous piece of Roman glassware that was probably made in Rome in around A.D. 5 to 25. It was made using a technique called cameo *(KAM ee oh)* glass. Cameo glass is made by using two layers of differently colored glass. For example, a bubble of blue glass is dipped into molten white glass. The two layers of glass are then blown together into a vase shape. Once the glass has cooled and hardened, the white layer is cut away to create an intricate raised design.

This celebrated piece of cameo glass was an important influence many centuries later, when the British potter Josiah Wedgwood made several copies of it to display a revolutionary new development in ceramics, called jasperware, in the 1780's. Wedgwood stoneware, which features a colored base and delicate white figures in a raised design, remains popular after more than 200 years.

LITERATURE AND LIBRARIES

Roman literature, written in **Latin**, was influenced by Greek poetry and drama. Such Roman writers as Plautus *(PLAW thus)*, who lived from around 254 to 184 B.C. and Terence *(TEHR uhns)*, who lived from around 190 to 159 B.C., modeled their comedies on Greek plays. An early Roman poet, Ennius *(EHN ee uhs)*, who lived from 239 to 169 B.C., wrote an **epic** *(EHP ihk)* poem about Rome called the *Annals*. Inspired by the work of Homer, who is traditionally considered to be the ancient Greek poet who composed the great epics the *Iliad* and the *Odyssey*, the *Annals* described the history of Rome from the founding of Rome to Ennius's own time.

Great Masters

A great deal of Roman literature reflects the Romans' interest in **rhetoric** *(REHT uhr ihk)*—the art of speaking and persuading. The ability to speak well in public, to impress and persuade, was very important for anyone who wanted to play a role in Roman political life. The influence of this rhetorical training is present in much Roman literature. Cicero *(SIHS uh ROH)*, who lived from 106 to 43 B.C., was a statesman who became one of the greatest masters of the Latin language. He wrote orations *(aw RAY shuhnz)*, or speeches, and works of **philosophy,** as well as many letters. During the reign of Augustus, the emperor took a personal interest in the work of two great Roman poets, Virgil (see box) and Horace, who lived from 65 to 8 B.C. Another poet, Ovid *(OV ihd)*, who lived from 43 B.C. to around A.D. 17, was best known for his witty and sophisticated love poems.

▲ A **fresco** portrait from Pompeii of a man and woman. They are both holding writing materials—the man clutches a papyrus scroll in his left hand; the woman holds a wax tablet and a stylus *(STY luhs),* which was used for writing on the wax.

◀ The ruins of the Library of Celsus in Ephesus *(EHF ih suhs)*, a city located in present-day Turkey that was under Roman rule in ancient times. This library was built early in the A.D. 100's as a huge tomb for the governor of the **province** of Asia. The governor's grave was beneath the ground floor. Above were stored more than 12,000 papyrus scrolls, making this one of the richest libraries in ancient times.

Writing It Down

In Roman times, writing was done in ink on scrolls made from **papyrus** *(puh PY ruhs)*. However, papyrus scrolls (which had to be made from fibers from the papyrus plant) were expensive. For everyday matters, people wrote on wax tablets, which could be wiped clean and used over again. Papyrus scrolls were gradually replaced by books with pages made of **parchment** (animal skin). This form of book was called a codex *(KOH dehks)*—the plural of codex is codices *(KOH duh seez)*. Parchment was stronger and smoother than papyrus, and books with pages were easier to read than long scrolls.

Following the example of the Greeks, the Romans built libraries for the storage of both papyrus scrolls and codices. Cicero had his own private library, and several emperors set up public libraries in Rome.

VIRGIL (70-19 B.C.)

Virgil *(VUHR juhl)*, whose full name was Publius Vergilius Maro *(POOB lee uhs vuhr JIHL ee uhs MAR oh)*, was born in northern Italy. He lived at a time of political turmoil, as the **Republic** came to an end and Augustus took power. Virgil's greatest work, the *Aeneid (ih NEE ihd)*, was modeled on Homer's *Iliad* and *Odyssey*. The *Iliad* tells about a portion of the **legendary** Trojan War between Greece and Troy. The *Odyssey* tells of the many adventures of the legendary Greek hero Odysseus *(oh DIHS ee uhs)*, known as Ulysses *(yoo LIHS eez)* in Latin, as he travels home from the war. The *Aeneid* describes the adventures of Aeneas *(ih NEE uhs)*, a legendary Trojan hero, but it also incorporates major events in Roman history.

POMPEII

Pompeii was an ancient Roman city located near the Bay of Naples—and less than a mile from the foot of Mount Vesuvius. It was a city of about 20,000 people, and it was popular with wealthy Romans, who built villas near the shore to enjoy the sunny climate. The site is well known today because when Mount Vesuvius erupted in A.D. 79, Pompeii and the neighboring cities of Stabiae (*STAY bee uh*) and Herculaneum (*HUR kyuh LAY nee uhm*) were all engulfed by cinders, ash, and stone. The buried remains of Pompeii lay almost completely undisturbed for many centuries, until excavations began in 1748. The ruins that have gradually been uncovered have provided huge amounts of information about how the Romans lived their daily lives.

The Roman Domus

Pompeii had many public buildings, including a **forum,** two theaters, and several temples. However, it is the excavation of the city's private homes that have given **archaeologists** some of the most valuable information about Roman life. The entrance hall of a typical Roman house, called a domus *(DOH mus)*, was the atrium *(AY tree uhm)*. The atrium—a rectangular space—was open to the sky. Any rain that fell through the roof opening in the atrium was caught in a shallow pool in the floor, called the impluvium *(ihm PLOO vee uhm)*. The atrium was the most public space in the house. A living room, called a tablinum *(TAB lih nuhm)*, linked the atrium to the private living quarters of the house. The private rooms were grouped around an open courtyard, called the peristyle *(PEHR uh styl)*. These rooms included a triclinium *(try KLIHN ee uhm)*, or dining room, and bedrooms. A few villas in Pompeii, belonging to the wealthiest owners, had their own bathhouses, with underfloor heating systems.

▲ **Frescoes** from the House of the Vettii in Pompeii. It is likely that this luxurious house was owned by two freedmen, the Vettii brothers. The frescoes are painted in a technique called trompe l'oeil *(tromp loy)*, which uses shadowing and other devices to make the viewer think the objects in a painting have three-dimensional depth.

FROZEN IN TIME

The eruption of Vesuvius happened so suddenly that the people of Pompeii were, in a sense, frozen in time. Over the centuries, the bodies of victims overwhelmed by the eruption have decomposed and left spaces in the solid ash that covered them. In the late 1800's, an Italian archaeologist named Giuseppe Fiorelli *(juh SEHP ee fee uh REHL ee)* developed a way to take casts of the bodies by pouring cement into these spaces. The casts allow us to see a copy of the body of someone who died in the eruption of Vesuvius (such as the person above). These casts serve as reminders of the terror experienced by the inhabitants of Pompeii as they were overcome by the poisonous gases and hot ash from the volcano.

The houses of the wealthy in Pompeii were large and beautifully decorated. The House of the Faun *(fawn)*—named after a **bronze** statue of a faun, or type of minor god of the fields and woods, found in the house—had two atria (the plural for atrium) and four triclinia, decorated with beautiful **mosaics**. In the House of the Vettii *(VEHT tee eye)*, delicate paintings covered the walls. However, the ordinary people of Pompeii lived in much smaller homes, often above or behind their shops.

FAMILY LIFE AND CHILDREN

The idea of the family was central to Roman society. The English word family comes from the **Latin** familia *(fuh MIHL ee uh)*, and the head of a Roman family was its oldest male member, the paterfamilias *(PAY tuhr fuh MIHL ee uhs)*, or "father of the family." The paterfamilias had control over his entire household, not only his wife and children, but also his slaves and often freedmen and women who were servants of the house. Under Roman law, the paterfamilias had absolute authority. He could choose to sell, abandon, or disown his children—or even have them put to death. He also chose suitable marriage partners for his sons and daughters. An adult son became a paterfamilias only when his own father died, and as long as his father lived, a son could not own property in his own right. In practice, however, most adult sons ruled their own families.

▲ A stone **relief** carving from the A.D. 100's depicts a family having a meal. The paterfamilias reclines on a couch, showing his position of superiority in the family.

Marriage

Among the Roman **nobility,** marriages were often made for political or financial reasons. For example, Julia, the daughter of Julius Caesar, was married to Pompey in 59 B.C. as part of the political scheming that led to the agreement to form the First Triumvirate (see pages 8-9). Girls could legally marry when they were 12 years old, and boys when they were 14. Many men, however, waited until they had started their careers before considering marriage. Consent was needed from the paterfamilias on both sides before a marriage could proceed.

The favorite time for Romans to get married was June, because that month was sacred to Juno, goddess of women. The groom and his family came to the bride's house, where the matron of honor (who had to be a woman who had married only once and remained married) linked the groom's and bride's right

WEDDING CLOTHES

A Roman bride wore very specific kinds of clothes for her marriage ceremony. Her dress was a simple white **tunic**, with a woollen belt tied in a special double knot, called a knot of Hercules. She wore an orange veil and cloak, and sandals of the same color. Her hair was divided into six locks, in a style worn by the Vestal Virgins.

hands as a symbol of their union. This was followed by an animal sacrifice, usually a pig. After the wedding feast, the bride was escorted—by the couple's friends and by three boys, one carrying a torch and the other two supporting her on either side—to the groom's house. When she reached the house, she performed various rituals, including touching both the hearth fire and water.

Children and Education

One of the main purposes of marriage was to provide children, particularly boys, to keep the family line going. Most children received their earliest education at home, often from well-educated Greek slaves. Middle-class boys were likely to receive instruction, but only upper-class girls were likely to be educated.

From the age of about 7 until 11, boys could attend school, where they learned reading, writing, and mathematics. Very few girls attended school. Most boys who continued their education past the age of 11 came from wealthy Roman families. They studied mainly Latin and Greek grammar and literature, as well as mathematics and astronomy. Even fewer went on to the next stage, where they studied the art of **rhetoric**.

▼ A relief sculpture from the A.D. 100's of children playing a game with walnuts.

CLOTHING

The basic garment worn by Roman men of all classes was a **tunic**, which generally went down to or just below the knees and was made of two pieces of cloth sewn together, with holes for the head and arms. A belt was worn around the middle. Poor people and slaves wore almost nothing else, but the better-off often wore a cloak in colder weather. The most common material for clothing was undyed wool, though some people had tunics made from linen. Silk, which was imported from Asia, was a luxury that only the very rich could afford.

The Toga

The formal dress for Roman male **citizens** was the toga. This was a large semicircular piece of cloth that was draped in folds over the top of the tunic. Most togas were made from wool, and they were heavy and cumbersome to wear. Ordinary Roman citizens wore undyed togas, but different colors and patterns were used to indicate status and rank. Freeborn boys wore a toga with a purple border, called the toga praetexta *(TOH guh pry TEHKS tuh)*, until they reached puberty, when they put on a plain toga to indicate their manhood. Generals returning from victorious campaigns wore the toga picta *(PIHK tuh)*, a highly decorated purple toga. People in mourning wore togas in dark colors, called toga pulla *(PUL luh)*. Men campaigning for public office wore a white toga (whitened with chalk), called the toga candida *(KAN dih duh)*. It was against the law for noncitizens to wear togas.

▶ A marble statue of a man wearing a toga. The toga was adopted by the Romans from clothing worn by the **Etruscans.** It became the dress of the upper classes because its weight and folds made it a difficult garment to wear for active physical labor—so a man wearing a toga was showing that he did not have to do hard physical work.

Women's Dress

The women's version of the tunic was the stola *(STOH luh)*, a long, loose garment that reached to the floor in folds. These garments could be dyed in bright colors, and those worn by wealthy women were made from such fine materials as linen, cotton, or even silk. A rectangular cloak, called a palla *(PAL luh)*, was sometimes worn over the top of the stola. Rich Roman women wore a great deal of jewelry, including earrings, necklaces, rings, bracelets, and anklets.

Wealthy Roman women had slaves to help them dress, to style their hair, and to apply their makeup. Over the centuries, Roman hairstyles ranged from the simple to the very elaborate. The most complicated styles were used during the reigns of the **Flavian** family of emperors, followed by the Emperor Trajan (reigned A.D. 98–117), when women wore their hair piled high on their heads in masses of curls. Some women wore wigs, made with blonde hair imported from the region that included what is present-day Germany.

▶ A Roman **fresco** of a woman pouring perfume into a flask. The painting shows the careful folds of the fine material of her stola, her jewelry, her elaborate hairstyle, and her delicate sandals.

ROADS AND TRANSPORTATION

The Romans built a transportation network across their **empire** that eventually spanned 50,000 miles (80,000 kilometers) of roads. These roads were initially constructed to allow the Roman army to move quickly and easily from one region to another. But they also became vital links for ordinary travelers, particularly traders and merchants. Trade flourished as such goods as food, silk, spices, gems, **ivory**, and wild animals were imported from across the Roman Empire and beyond. The roads were also important for communications between Rome and its **provinces**. The Romans developed the fastest postal system—the cursus publicus *(KUR suhs POOB lih kuhs)*— of the ancient world. For use only by the emperor and his officials and friends, this system relied on a series of messengers on horseback who typically traveled about 50 miles (80 kilometers) in a day—though they could go faster in a crisis.

▲ A section of the Via Appia, the major road leading into Rome from the south.

A Roman Road

Roman roads were noted for how very straight they were—these roads went over such obstacles as hills rather than around them. The roads were very carefully constructed, with the result that many sections of Roman roads have survived to the present day. To build a road, the Romans first laid a foundation made from rubble or large stones. The foundation was covered with a layer of concrete. Some roads were paved with stone slabs. All Roman roads sloped from the center to either side to allow water to drain off. The first major Roman road, begun in

312 B.C., was the Via Appia (Appian Way), which ran southeast from Rome. At first it extended 132 miles (212 kilometers) to the town of Capua, but eventually it was extended another 230 miles (370 kilometers) to Tarentum and Brundisium *(bruhn DEE zee uhm)*—the present-day city of Brindisi *(BREEN dee zee)*, near the southern tip of Italy.

ROMAN LIGHTHOUSES

When the Emperor Claudius built a new harbor at Portus, he ordered the construction of a lighthouse to guide ships as they neared land. A huge ship was filled with concrete and sunk to form the base of this lighthouse. A fire was kept burning on the top, to act as a light. Nothing remains of this lighthouse, but another Roman lighthouse, the Tower of Hercules (left) in present-day La Coruña *(lah kawr OO nyah)*, Spain, is still in use and is the world's oldest operational lighthouse.

Water Travel

Sea trade flourished under Roman rule. Rome's main port during the **Republic** was Ostia *(OS tee uh)*, about 15 miles (25 kilometers) downriver from Rome, where the Tiber flows into the sea. But because Ostia's harbor was too shallow for large ships, the Emperor Claudius built a new port nearby, named Portus. The biggest merchant ships had large square sails. These ships were steered using a pair of large oars at the stern (back) of the ship. Smaller ships had a triangular sail. The largest ships measured up to 180 feet (55 meters) long and 45 feet (14 meters) wide, and they could carry hundreds of tons of cargo. The Roman navy, initially developed during the First Punic War, used warships called galleys *(GAL eez)*, with square sails and rows of oarsmen down both sides.

FOOD

The Romans ate almost everything—including large **dormice** especially bred for eating. Cereals, mainly wheat and barley, were made into many different types of bread and also into porridge. From the condition of some skeletons from Pompeii that were studied by scientists, it is clear that the poorest in society, and some slaves, struggled to exist on a diet of thin porridge. For most ordinary people, however, the basic diet was based on more generous amounts of cereals, olive oil, and vegetables. The Romans produced and ate such vegetables as lentils, beans, radishes, celery, lettuce, cabbage, onions, and garlic. Honey was used as a sweetener. Garum *(GAIR uhm)*, a type of sauce made from fish and olive oil, was very popular and was used to flavor many dishes. Meat was expensive, so except for the wealthy, most people ate only modest amounts. Pork was the most common meat.

Food Imports

As Roman power spread, new foods were imported into Rome from all over the **empire** and beyond. Such spices as pepper, nutmeg, and cloves came from Asia, and such fruits as pomegranates *(POM GRAN ihts)* and dates were imported from North Africa. The rapid growth of Rome's population meant that the city could no longer get adequate quantities of food from the surrounding countryside. Romans came to rely on imports of such staples as wheat from their conquered territories, mainly Sicily, Egypt, and other parts of North Africa.

▼ A **fresco** from one of the smaller houses in Pompeii depicts bread being distributed.

◄ A **mosaic** showing partridges hanging from a rope. The Romans may have hung game birds in this manner to "age" the meat. The mosaic was part of a decorated dining room floor in a Roman house in North Africa.

A Roman Dinner Party

While ordinary people ate quite simply, rich Romans showed off their wealth by using exotic ingredients in elaborate dishes. All Romans ate their main meal of the day, the cena *(SEE nuh)*, in the early evening after the day's work was done. Those who could afford it reclined on couches that ran around three sides of a table to eat, leaning on the left arm and eating with the right hand. A dinner party at a wealthy Roman household might consist of appetizers of eggs, olives, and shellfish, followed by up to seven main courses and a dessert of fruit and nuts. The main courses included fish, meat, and game birds, often served in spicy sauces.

POTTERY HILL

Monte Testaccio *(MOHN tay tehs TAH chee oh)* is a hill on the banks of the Tiber in Rome that is entirely artificial. Some 160 feet (50 meters) high, Monte Testaccio consists of the remains of pottery jars—known as amphorae—that were used to import olive oil to ancient Rome. The oil came from the Baetica *(BY tih kuh)* region—modern-day Andalusia *(an duh LOO zhuh)* in southern Spain—and from northern Africa. Amphorae were used to store and transport such goods as oil, wine, and garum. Once the contents of the amphorae had been transferred into smaller containers, the amphorae were broken up and dumped.

SPORT AND SPECTACLE

The Romans loved bloodthirsty spectacles—at the Colosseum in Rome, crowds of up to 50,000 people came to watch **gladiators** (trained fighters) fight each other or battle against wild beasts. The rival attraction to these events was chariot racing.

Gladiators

Combat between gladiators was originally an **Etruscan** tradition. Fights between captives or slaves were held at the funerals of dead warriors to please the spirits of the dead. The first gladiator games were held in Rome in 264 B.C. at the funeral of an aristocrat. Most of the subsequent games were held in association with funerals or as state occasions; these events were usually paid for by the emperor. Rome's Colosseum was one of many **amphitheaters** built to stage such spectacles all over the **empire.**

▼ In the lower half of this **mosaic** from the A.D. 300's, a retarius has thrown his net over his opponent, a heavily armed Samnite gladiator. The Samnite, however, seems unbothered by the net, and in the top image the retarius lies wounded on the ground.

Most gladiators were slaves, prisoners of war, or condemned criminals, though some freedmen chose to train and fight as gladiators. There were even a few women gladiators. Gladiator training schools were established all over Italy and in many other parts of the empire. There were several different types of gladiators, depending on their weapons and styles of fighting. The retarius *(ray TAHR ee uhs)*, or net man, was armed with a net and a three-pronged spear. The Thracian—named for Thrace, a large region in the Balkan Peninsula—carried a round shield and curved sword. The murmillo *(MOOR mih loh)*—who may have been called that for his fish-shaped helmet (the word *murmillo* derived from the Greek word for fish)—and the **Samnite** fighters were both more heavily armed with big shields and stabbing swords. Gladiators usually fought until one was killed or the loser surrendered. In the latter case, it was then up to the spectators, and in Rome the emperor, to decide whether the loser should be killed. Gladiators also fought wild animals. Many thousands of animals were imported into Rome for these spectacles. At the first games held in the Colosseum, in A.D. 80, some 5,000 animals were killed.

Chariot Races

Chariot racing took place on an oval track called a circus. There were racetracks all over the empire, but the best known was the Circus Maximus in Rome. Roman charioteers raced for one of four teams—red, white, blue, and green—each with its own loyal supporters. The Circus Maximus track was more than 2,000 feet (610 meters) long, with a barrier, called the spina *(SPEE nuh)*, down the middle. The chariots, often pulled by teams of four horses, raced seven laps around the spina. The number of laps run was recorded by removing large wooden eggs or turning over **bronze** dolphin statues that decorated the spina.

ANIMAL HUNTS

The Romans became very efficient at hunting and capturing wild animals for export to Rome. The animals came from all parts of the empire and beyond. Panthers and tigers came from western Asia; hippopotamuses and crocodiles from Egypt; and lions, elephants, and ostriches from northern Africa. This trade devastated the wildlife of these regions, and by the A.D. 300's, it was increasingly difficult to fulfill the demand for animals.

▲ Chariot racing was exciting, but very dangerous. In a seven-lap race, each charioteer tried to take the best position nearest to the spina, but skill was needed to avoid a crash. If the wheel of the chariot touched the spina, it could shatter, sending the chariot out of control.

THEATER, MUSIC, AND DANCE

Roman theater developed from Greek origins, and many of the actors were Greek. Theater performances did not draw the huge crowds attracted by the games or the races, but comic theater was nevertheless very popular.

Theaters

Roman theaters usually had banked seats—much like the seats in modern movie theaters. The banked seats were in a semicircle, so that everyone in the audience could see the stage. The stage was slightly raised, with a back wall that was often decorated with **columns** and statues. There were three openings in the back wall of the stage for actors to make their entrances and exits, and often two further openings at the sides. Theaters were open to the skies, but an awning was often erected across the roof to shade the audience from the sun.

▲ The Roman theater at Bosra, in present-day Syria, is one of the best preserved in the world. It was built sometime around A.D. 150 to 200, when Bosra was the capital of the Roman **province** of Arabia. The theater was covered by silk awnings to provide shelter from the sun during the summer and from rain in the winter. The actors made their entrances and exits through openings at the back and sides of the stage.

THE THEATER OF MARCELLUS
Started by Julius Caesar and completed by Augustus Caesar in 13 B.C., the semicircular, enclosed Theater of Marcellus *(mar CELL us)* was the largest in Rome. Much of it still stands. It was turned into a palazzo (mansion) in the 1500's and is today a luxury apartment building.

Mime and Pantomime

Above all, the Romans loved **mime** and **pantomime**. Roman mimes were dramatic entertainments that presented scenes from everyday life in a ridiculous and often strange manner. Both men and women took part in these crowd-pleasing performances. Some performances even featured the actual executions of convicted criminals. From the mime (in which the actors spoke and did not use masks), the Romans developed pantomime, which became very popular during the **empire.** In a pantomime performance, a single dancer—the pantomimus *(pahn toh MEE muhs)*—used masks and costumes to act out various characters without speaking, accompanied by an orchestra and a chorus. The musicians played such instruments as flutes, pipes, trumpets, and cymbals. The chorus sang or recited heroic tales as the dancer moved.

Music

Music played an important part at such events as religious and state ceremonies, **gladiatorial** games, and theater performances. Wealthy people hired musicians and dancers to entertain them, and bands of musicians performed in the streets of Rome. Most musical instruments played by the Romans were of Greek origin. The double pipes, called auloi *(OW loh ee)* by the Greeks and tibiae *(TIHB ee ee)* by the Romans, were made of wood, bone, or metal. Each pipe had three or four holes that were covered and uncovered by the fingers and had a reed in its mouthpiece. The lyre *(lyr)*, called the cithara *(SIHTH uhr uh)* by the Romans, was another popular instrument. Harplike, the lyre's strings were plucked. It was often used to accompany singing.

▼ A **mosaic** from the Villa of Cicero in Pompeii depicts a group of musicians. The woman on the left is playing double pipes, the man in the center clashes small cymbals, and the man on the right plays a tambourine. The figures are masked, suggesting that they are taking part in a comic entertainment.

DECLINE AND FALL

The huge size of the Roman **Empire** was the main factor that led to its decline and ultimate downfall. As time went on, it became increasingly difficult for one person to rule such a vast area. Soldiers serving in the Roman armies in the far-flung regions of the empire often felt far greater loyalty to their commanders than to the emperor back in Rome. Between A.D. 235 and 284, there were 19 different emperors, many of them army commanders whose troops had named them emperor. These power struggles left the empire weak and unable to withstand various attacks from the **Germanic** tribes to the north or the **Persians** to the east.

Diocletian and Constantine

When Diocletian became emperor in A.D. 284, he tried to stabilize the empire by reorganizing the way it was ruled. He divided the empire into two halves, each half to be ruled by a senior and a junior emperor. Under this tetrarchy *(TEHT rahr kee)*, or rule of four, Diocletian was senior emperor of the east while his co-emperor in the west was Maximian

▼ The division of the Roman world into the West Roman Empire and the East Roman Empire became permanent after the death of the Emperor Theodosius *(THEE uh DOH shee uhs)* in A.D. 395. The eastern part flourished as the Byzantine *(BIHZ uhn teen)* Empire for another thousand years, but the western part fell in less than a century, after successive attacks from various Germanic peoples.

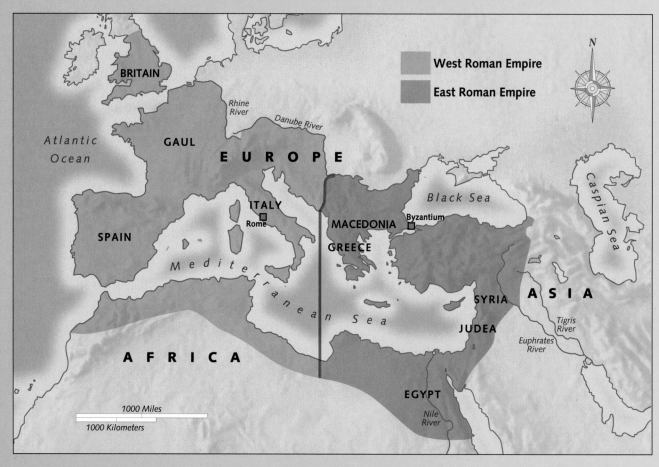

CONSTANTINE THE GREAT

Constantine I was born in about A.D. 275. His father, Constantius *(kahn STAN chee uhs)*, was emperor of the West Roman Empire, and when he died in 306, the army proclaimed Constantine as his successor. Civil war broke out as other claimants to the throne struggled for power. In 312, Constantine defeated his main rival, Maxentius *(mak SEHN chee uhs)*. Constantine later said that before this battle he saw a cross (the symbol of Jesus Christ) shining in the sky. After his victory, Constantine became a strong supporter of Christianity. He was baptized a Christian as he lay on his deathbed, in 337.

▲ A **relief** sculpture carved out of rock at Naqsh-e Rustam *(NUHK shee ROOS tuhm)* in present-day Iran shows the Persian King Shapur I *(shah POOR;* reigned A.D. 241–272) in triumph over the Roman Emperor Valerian *(vuh LIHR ee uhn)*. Shapur defeated Valerian at Edessa *(eh DESS uh;* in the south of modern-day Turkey). The emperor remained a captive until the end of his life.

(mak SIHM ee an). When Diocletian retired in A.D. 305, however, there were further power struggles. Eventually, Constantine came to power and united the empire once again. Constantine made Christianity the chief religion of the Roman Empire in A.D. 325. For strategic reasons, he also established a new capital at Byzantium *(bih ZAHN tee uhm)*, which became known as Constantinople *(kahn stan tih NOH puhl)*—present-day Istanbul, Turkey. Byzantium was closer to the frontier regions of the Danube and Euphrates rivers (in southeastern Europe and southwestern Asia, respectively); it was also at the center of several trade routes. Although Rome remained an important and hugely wealthy city, it was no longer the political center of the empire.

After the death of Constantine in 337 there was once again a bitter power struggle. By 395, the empire was permanently divided into two parts, the West Roman Empire with its capital in Rome, and the East Roman Empire with its capital at Constantinople. The western part of the empire was attacked by Germanic peoples, including the Vandals *(VAN duhlz)* and the Visigoths *(VIHZ uh goths)*. The Visigoths plundered Rome in 410, and the Vandals looted the city in 455. The West Roman Empire finally collapsed in 476, when a German chief named Odoacer *(OH doh AY suhr)* forced the last Roman emperor, Romulus Augustulus *(aw GUHS tuh luhs)*, from the throne. The eastern part, known as the Byzantine Empire, flourished until 1453.

THE ROMAN LEGACY

The Roman **Empire** may have disintegrated many centuries ago, but its legacy lives on in the modern world in many different ways. The Romans and their achievements have had a huge influence on the development of Western **civilization**. The **Latin** language is the basis of several European languages, Roman law is still studied at modern universities, and people all over Europe and beyond continue to travel along the routes of Roman roads—and in some cases over actual Roman roads and bridges still in existence.

Alphabet and Language

The Romans developed their alphabet from the one used by the **Etruscans**. Today, the Roman alphabet is the most widely used writing system in the world. The alphabet used by the Romans had 23 letters; the letters J, U, and W were added in the Middle Ages (the period of European

▲ The design of the interior of Union Station in Washington, D.C., completed in 1907, was modeled by architect Daniel Burnham on the great Baths of Diocletian in Rome. The station's barrel-**vaulted** ceiling is 96 feet (29 meters) high and is adorned with gold.

history that followed the fall of the West Roman Empire, from about the 400's through the 1400's). The Latin language remained the language of religion and scholarship through the Middle Ages, and the forms of Latin spoken in various parts of the former empire formed the basis for the development of French, Italian, Spanish, Portuguese, and Romanian. Together with some other dialects, these are known as the **Romance languages**. Many other languages, including English, make use of words that are derived from Latin roots.

Law, Government, and Church

Roman law provides the model for the legal systems of many countries, and many modern governments reflect the Roman political system. The U.S. government, for example, is modeled in part on that of the Roman **Republic,** and one of the branches of Congress is called the **Senate.** Roman coins, which bore a picture of the emperor on one side, have also influenced the design of modern coins. The Roman Catholic Church still has its base in Rome, and during the Middle Ages, it replaced the Roman Empire as the unifying force in Europe.

Architecture and Engineering

The fact that many Roman bridges, **aqueducts,** and buildings are still standing and in some cases still in use today is evidence of the high standards of Roman engineering. The styles of Roman architecture have also been a major influence. Many architects have used Roman models as the basis of the designs for their buildings. Triumphal arches, built by the Roman emperors to celebrate their victories, have also been copied in many cities of the world, including London's Marble Arch, the Arc de Triomphe *(ahrk duh tree AWNF)* of Paris, and New York City's Washington Square Arch.

▶ The Arc de Triomphe in Paris, France, is the largest triumphal arch in the world. It was commissioned by the French Emperor Napoleon I in 1806 to commemorate his victorious campaigns. Its design is based on the Arch of Constantine in Rome, which had been built to commemorate a military victory by the Emperor Constantine in A.D. 312. The Arch of Constantine still stands near the Colosseum.

THE ETERNAL CITY

The ancient city of Rome fell into ruin and disrepair after the end of the West Roman Empire in A.D. 476. Today, however, Rome is recognized as one of the world's most beautiful and historic cities. The remains of ancient Rome sit alongside architectural masterpieces from the Renaissance and later periods of history. A city of more than 2.5 million people, Rome is the capital of Italy. Because of its long and eventful history, it is often called the Eternal City.

GLOSSARY

alliance A union formed by agreement, joining the interests of people or states.

amphitheater A circular or oval building with rows of seats that rise around a central open space, called the arena.

aqueduct An artificial channel through which water is taken to the place where it will be used.

archaeologist A scientist who studies the remains of past human cultures.

artisan A person skilled in some industry or trade.

auxiliary A noncitizen soldier in the Roman army. These soldiers often had specialized skills, such as fighting with slings, with bows and arrows, or on horseback.

bronze A metal made mostly of copper and tin.

citizen In ancient Rome, a person who enjoyed rights and privileges under Roman law that were forbidden to noncitizens.

city-state An independent state consisting of a city and the territories depending on it.

civil law A custom or law that covers such noncriminal matters as contracts, ownership of property, and payment for personal injury.

civilization The way of life in a society that features complex economic, governmental, and social systems.

colony A territory inhabited by people who leave their own country and settle in another land; the territory is usually distant from the country that governs it.

column A slender, upright structure, such as a pillar or post; a column may be either free-standing or used as a support.

confederation A league or **alliance**.

consul During the time of the Roman **Republic,** one of the two chief **magistrates** who were elected every year to head the government.

deity A god.

dictator During the **Republic,** a supreme **magistrate** who was appointed at times of emergency to perform a specific task.

divination Trying to learn about the future by magical or super-natural means.

dormouse A rodent, related to mice and rats, that resembles a small squirrel. Plural: dormice.

empire A group of nations or states under one ruler or government. The Roman Empire began in 27 B.C., with the collapse of the **Republic** and the reign of the first Roman emperor, Augustus.

epic A long poem that tells of the adventures of one or more great heroes.

equites In the **Republic,** men who served in the army as cavalrymen. By the time of the Roman **Empire,** the equites were second in rank only to senators.

Etruscans An ancient people who lived in Etruria, which is in the present-day regions of Tuscany, Umbria, and Latium in modern Italy.

Flavian Having to do with members of the Flavius family of ancient Rome, especially the three Roman emperors Vespasian and his two sons, Titus and Domitian.

forum In ancient Rome and other towns and cities under Roman control, the public square and marketplace where business was done and where public assemblies were held.

fresco A painting made on damp plaster, using pigments mixed with water.

Gauls A people who occupied a region called Gaul that now includes France, Belgium, Luxembourg, and parts of the Netherlands, Germany, and Switzerland.

Germanic Referring to ancient tribes from areas located in modern-day Britain, Germany, and Scandinavia.

gladiator A trained warrior who fought bloody battles with other gladiators or against wild animals to entertain spectators.

ivory A hard substance that makes up the main part of the tusks and teeth of certain animals. The tusks of the African elephant are the major source of ivory. Other ivory comes from tusks of the walrus, narwhal, and fossilized prehistoric mammoths and from teeth of the hippopotamus and sperm whale.

Latin A native or inhabitant of the region of ancient Latium or of ancient Rome; the language spoken by the ancient Romans.

legend A folk story, often set in the past, which may be based in truth but which may also contain fictional or fantastic elements. Legends are similar to myths, but myths often are about such sacred topics as gods or the creation of the world.

legion A unit of the Roman army containing several thousand men.

Macedonia An ancient kingdom that covered all of the modern country that is also called Macedonia, plus parts of northern Greece and southwestern Bulgaria.

magistrate A government official.

manumission The formal release of a person from slavery.

mime A dramatic entertainment that presented scenes from everyday life in a ridiculous way.

mosaic A design or picture that is made by pressing small pieces of colored glass or stone into a soft mortar.

mythology A body of sacred stories about such topics as gods and the creation of the world.

noble and **nobility** A person or persons of high standing in their culture.

pantomime A theatrical performance in which a single dancer used masks and costumes to act out various characters without speaking, accompanied by an orchestra and a chorus.

papyrus A tall plant that grows in water or very wet soil. Also the material for writing on that was made from fibers of the papyrus plant by the ancient Egyptians, Greeks, and Romans.

parchment Animal skin that has been treated for writing on.

patrician A person from a wealthy, aristocratic family in ancient Rome.

pediment The low triangular part on the front of a building, usually just below a slanted roof.

Persians A people who lived in the north of Mesopotamia, which included parts of what are now Iran and Afghanistan.

plebeian A person of common birth in ancient Rome.

philosophy The study of human nature and such ideas as the meaning of life and the best way to live.

Phoenicians A people who lived in the area made up of the coastal regions of present-day Syria, Lebanon, and Israel.

province A division of a country or **empire.**

relief A sculpture in which the figures or designs project from their background.

republic A state in which **citizens** elect representatives to run the government.

rhetoric The art of using words in speech or writing to persuade.

Romance languages A group of languages that developed from **Latin** and are spoken in places that were once part of the Roman **Empire.** They include French, Italian, Portuguese, Romanian, and Spanish.

Sabines An ancient people who lived northeast of Rome in present-day Umbria, Italy.

Samnites An ancient tribe in what is now southern Italy.

Senate In ancient Rome, the council that advised the king, **consuls,** or emperor.

Sibylline Books A collection of prophecy, which in Roman **legend** had been written by a sibyl *(SIHB uhl),* a woman supposedly able to tell the future. In times of difficulty or crisis, the Romans consulted the Sibylline Books.

tenement A building that is divided into sets of rooms for different families to live in, especially in a poor section of a town or city.

terra cotta A type of baked clay often used in fine art, building decoration, and as a construction material.

tribune In ancient Rome, an official elected by the **plebeians** to represent their interests.

tunic A loose, short piece of clothing that is slipped on over the head and is often belted at the waist.

vault An arched roof or ceiling.

ADDITIONAL RESOURCES

Books

Ancient Rome
by Jane Bingham (World Almanac Library, 2006)

Ancient Rome
by Peter Chrisp (Dorling Kindersley, 2006)

Ancient Rome: Revealed
by Peter Chrisp (Dorling Kindersley, 2003)

Cultural Atlas for Young People: Ancient Rome
by Mike Corbishley (Chelsea House, 2007)

Eyewitness: Ancient Rome
by Simon James (Dorling Kindersley, 2004)

Handbook to Life in Ancient Rome
by Lesley Adkins and Roy A. Adkins (Facts on File, 2004)

Julius Caesar: Roman General and Statesman
by Don Nardo (Compass Point Books, 2009)

World History: The Roman Empire
by Don Nardo (Lucent Books, 2005)

The Roman Empire
by Don Nardo (Lucent Books, 2006)

Web Sites

http://www.ancientworlds.net/aw/City/11

http://www.bbc.co.uk/schools/romans/

http://www.metmuseum.org/toah/hi/te_index.asp?i=20

http://www.pbs.org/empires/romans/

http://www.roman-empire.net/index.html

http://www.unrv.com

INDEX

Aegean Sea 20
Africa 4, 6–7, 39, 51
    imports from 19, 50, 53
Agriculture 17–19
Alliances 8, 14
Alphabet 58
Alps 5, 7
Amphitheaters 4, 22–23, 30, 35, 52
Animals 24
    domestic 18, 27
    wild 22, 25, 48, 52–53
Apothecaries 16
Aqueducts 30, 32–33, 59
Archaeologists 4, 13, 42–43
Architecture 30–35, 58–59
Armor 15, 38
Army 4, 7–9, 21, 48
    life in the 14–15, 18, 56
    organization of 10, 15
Art 36–38
Artisans 38–39
Asia 4, 8, 41, 46, 50, 53
Astronomy 33, 45
Augustus (emperor) 5, 16, 24, 29, 54
    army under 14–15
    Rome under 9, 11, 40–41
Auxiliaries 14

Baths 13, 30, 32, 35, 37, 42
Britain 4, 13, 38
Byzantine Empire 56–57

Calendars 28-29
Caligula (emperor) 11, 17
Capital punishment see Execution
Capitoline Hill 6, 24, 26
Caracalla (emperor) 13, 35
Carthage 5–7
Chariot racing 35, 52–53
Children 13, 17, 20, 44–45
Christians 22–23, 26, 35, 57
Cicero (statesman) 40–41
Circus Maximus 35, 53
Citizens 13–14, 23, 46
City-states 6, 8
Claudius (emperor) 17, 49
Cleopatra (queen of Egypt) 9
Clothing 44, 46–47
Colosseum 4, 32, 35, 52, 59

Concrete 31–32
Constantine (emperor) 5, 26, 46, 57, 59
Consuls 7, 10–12, 16
Crassus (general) 9
Crime see Law
Crops 18–19, 50

Dacia 8, 15
Diocletian (emperor) 35, 56–57

Education 45
Egypt 4, 9, 50
Elephants 7, 53
Engineering 32–33, 59
Entertainment 23, 35, 52–55
Equites 13
Etruscans 6–7, 36, 46, 52, 58
Europe 4–5, 8, 57
Execution 22–23, 26, 55

Family life 44–45
Farming see Agriculture
Festivals 26, 28–29
Fire (dangers of) 35
Food 50–51
Forum 6, 15, 22, 34
Fresco (painting) 7, 28, 47
    examples from Pompeii 27, 37, 40,
        42, 50
Funerals 52

Galleys (ships) 20–21, 49
Games
    children's 45
    public 11, 26, 30, 52–53
Gaul 18-19, 39
Gauls (people) 7
Germanic tribes 9, 56–57
Gladiators 21–22, 52
Glassmaking 38–39
Goddesses 13, 17, 38, 44
    worship of 24–25, 27
Gods 28–31, 34, 43
    worship of 24–25, 27
Governors 9, 23, 41
Greeks 6–8, 45
    artistic influence of 36
    cultural influence of 24, 30, 33,
        40–41, 54–55

Hadrian (emperor) 31, 46
Hairstyles 46–47
Hannibal (general) 7
Homer (poet) 40–41
Horace (poet) 40
Housing 35, 42–43
    see also Villas

Imprisonment 23
Italian peninsula 4–7, 24

Jewelry 38, 47
Julia Agrippina (empress) 17
Julius Caesar (emperor) 5, 9, 28–29,
    44, 54
Justinian (emperor) 23

Latin (language) 28, 40, 44–45, 58
Latins (people) 4, 6
Law 12–13, 20, 22–23, 29, 58–59
    and marriage 17
    and order 8
    religious 26
Legends 4, 25, 41
Legionaries 15
Libraries 41
Literature 40–41, 45
Livia Drusilla (empress) 16

Macedonia 8
Magistrates 10–11, 21, 23
Marcus Aurelius (emperor) 26, 36
Mark Antony (general) 9
Marriage 12, 17, 44–45
Mediterranean Sea 5, 21, 38–39
Metalwork 38
Mime and pantomime 55
Mining 20–21
Mosaic 13, 37, 39, 43
    examples of 19, 21, 51, 55
Music 55

Nero (emperor) 11, 17
Nerva (emperor) 32

Octavian see Augustus
Ovid (poet) 40

Painting 36–37, 43, 46
see also Fresco
Palatine Hill 6, 24, 35
Pantheon 30–31
Papyrus 40–41
Patricians 12–13, 22
Pax Romana 5, 9
Persians 56–57
Pertinax (emperor) 21
Plebeians 12–13, 22
Pliny the Elder (writer) 33
Plutarch (writer) 29
Poets 40
Pompeii 22, 25, 27, 42–43
artifacts recovered from 37–38, 40, 50, 55
Pompey (general) 9, 44
Pont du Gard (bridge) 32–33
Pottery 39, 51
Praetorian Guard 11, 15
Praetors 11
Priestesses 17
Priests 10, 12, 26–27, 29
Provinces 8–9, 39, 48, 54
Ptolemy (astronomer) 33
Punic Wars 5–8, 18, 49

Quaestors 10–11

Relief (sculpture) 36
Republic 4–5, 17, 26, 34, 59
early 7, 12, 18
end of the 9, 11, 41
Rhetoric 40, 45
Roads 4, 6, 30, 48–49, 58
Romulus and Remus 5, 25

Sabines 6, 13
Sacrifice 26–27, 45
Samnites 6–7, 52
Science 33
Sculpture 36–37, 46
Senate 5, 10–11, 29, 34,
U.S. government 59
Senators 10, 13, 16
Sewage 34
Ships 49
see also Galleys
Sibylline Books 26
Sicily 6, 8, 50
Slaves 13, 17–18, 22–23, 44, 52
living conditions of 20–21, 50
roles of 45, 47
Social class 12–13, 17, 20–22
and clothing 46
and education 45
and food 50–51
and housing 43

Spartacus (slave leader) 21–22

Taxes 8, 12
Temples 27, 30–31, 34, 42
Theater 42, 54–55
Theodosius (emperor) 56
Thrace 21, 52
Tiber River 4, 6, 34, 49
Tiberius (emperor) 11, 16
Togas 25, 46
Trade 6, 20, 39, 48–50, 57
Trajan (emperor) 5, 8–9, 15, 47
Tribunes 12
Triumvirate, First 9, 44
Tunics 36, 44, 46–47

Valerian (emperor) 57
Vestal Virgins 17, 26, 44
Vesuvius, Mount 21–22, 37, 42-43
Villas 13, 18, 37, 42
Virgil (poet) 40–41

Weapons 15, 38, 52
Weddings 44–45
Wine 19, 21, 39
Women 13, 16–17, 44–45, 52
Writers 19, 29, 33, 40–41
Writing materials 40–41

Acknowledgments

The Art Archive: 5, 7, 26, 46 (Museo Capitolino Rome/Gianni Dagli Orti), 10, 22, 30, 42 (Gianni Dagli Orti), 11 (Staatliche Glypothek, Munich/Alfredo Dagli Orti), 12 (Musée du Louvre, Paris/Gianni Dagli Orti), 13 (Jarrold Publishing), 16, 28, 44, 45 (Museo della Civilta Romana, Rome/Gianni Dagli Orti), 18 (Musée Luxembourgeois, Arlon, Belgium/Gianni Dagli Orti), 19 (Archaeological Museum, Cherchel, Algeria/Gianni Dagli Orti), 20 (Archaeological Museum, Istanbul/Gianni Dagli Orti), 21, 51 (Bardo Museum, Tunis/Gianni Dagli Orti), 23, 54 (Manuel Cohen), 1, 27, 40, 50, 55 (Archaeological Museum, Naples/Alfredo Dagli Orti), 29, 38 (Archaeological Museum, Naples/Gianni Dagli Orti), 37 (Villa of the Mysteries, Pompeii/Alfredo Dagli Orti), 41 (Alfredo Dagli Orti), 47 (Museo Nazionale Terme, Rome/Gianni Dagli Orti), 52 (Archaeological Museum, Madrid/Gianni Dagli Orti), 57; **Bridgeman Art Library:** 35 (private collection), 39 (The British Museum, London); **Corbis:** 14 (MGM/The Kobal Collection), 15 (Alinari Archives), 33 (Bettmann), 36 (Paul Seheult/Eye Ubiquitous), 49 (Alan Copson/JAI), 58 (Kelly-Mooney Photography); **Shutterstock:** 4 (Bryan Busovicki), 31 (Roca), 32 (MDD), 34 (Motordigitaal), 59 (Jonathan Larsen); **Werner Forman Archive:** 9, 17 (The British Museum, London), 24 (Antiquario Palatino, Rome), 25, 48 (no photographer credited), 43 (Pompeii Museum).

Cover image: **Alamy Images** (Peter Christopher)
Back cover image: **Shutterstock** (Joop Snijder, Jr.)